Steinbeck's

GRAPES OF WRATH

CHARLOTTE ALEXANDER
DEPARTMENT OF ENGLISH
NEW YORK UNIVERSITY

MONARCH
PRESS

Published by
MONARCH PRESS
a Simon & Schuster division of
Gulf & Western Corporation
Simon & Schuster Building
1230 Avenue of the Americas
New York, N.Y. 10020

MONARCH PRESS and colophon are trademarks
of Simon & Schuster, registered in the U.S. Patent
and Trademark Office.

Standard Book Number: 0-671-00692-4

Library of Congress Catalog Card Number: 66-1737

Printed in the United States of America.

CONTENTS

INTRODUCTION

A BIOGRAPHICAL SKETCH: John Steinbeck was born in 1902 in the town of Salinas, California. It is generally agreed that the most significant biographical link between Steinbeck and his writings is this fact of his birth and growth to maturity in the Salinas Valley: here is the source of his knowledge and love of nature, his biological view of life (explained below), and many of his characters, whether paisanos and bums of *Tortilla Flat, Cannery Row* and *Sweet Thursday* or migrant workers of *In Dubious Battle, Of Mice and Men* and *The Grapes of Wrath.*

STEINBECK'S BOYHOOD: Steinbeck lived most of his first forty years in the Salinas Valley, where his mother taught in the public schools of the area and his father was for many years treasurer of Monterey County. (It is said that the author's early novels were written in discarded double-entry ledgers.) Steinbeck's boyhood was probably much like that of Jody in one of his most popular stories, "The Red Pony." At that time the "long valley" was a series of small farms devoted to cattle raising and the growing of fruit and vegetables, among which were interspersed little towns where the farmers brought their produce to market; young Steinbeck worked during school vacations for the neighboring farmers and ranchers. Surely these early years of life close to nature form the background from which Steinbeck draws his detailed—and often beautiful—descriptions of natural phenomena. That he attaches importance to these youthful experiences in nature can be seen in the following anecdote: at the request of a publisher for early biographical facts Steinbeck replied that the most important items would probably be of little significance to others; for example, ". . . the way the sparrows hopped about on the mud street early in the morning when I was little. . . . the most tremendous morning in the world when my pony had a colt."

EARLY LITERARY INFLUENCES AND EFFORTS: At the same time, in addition to living close to nature as a youth, it is clear that Steinbeck read widely, probably through the influence of his schoolteacher mother. Through his fictional characters and other channels (such as correspondence) he has indicated a wide range of reading interests: Walter Scott, Jack London, Robert Louis Stevenson; Dostoyevsky's *Crime and Punishment,* Flaubert's *Madame Bovary,* Hardy's *The Return of the Native.* And it is interesting that he has commented of such reading, "certain books . . . were realer than experience. . . . I read all of these books when I was very young and I remember them not at all as books but as things that happened to me." Such remarks reveal Steinbeck's constant emphasis in his writings upon the concrete and experiential rather than the abstract and theoretical. Steinbeck has also manifested an interest in non-fictional universally great books, such as the Bible, philosophical literature of ancient India, and Greek historians.

HIS ENVIRONMENT AS SOURCE MATERIAL: Although he contributed to literary publications both in high school and college (he attended Stanford University for five years as an English major, without taking a degree), the entire period of his young adulthood was intermixed with many experiences in the laboring world. Before beginning courses at Stanford he worked as an assistant chemist in a sugar-beet factory nearby. During the intervals of attendance at Stanford he was employed on ranches and road-building gangs. All of this experience provided firsthand observation of the attitudes, manners and language of the working man, as well as the foundation of his sympathy with the situation of such laborers. Even during a brief stay in New York City (1925-1927), at which point he seems definitely to have decided on a career of writing, since he made unsuccessful attempts to publish stories, he worked both as a newspaper reporter and a laborer, and he financed his return to California by shipping as a deck hand via the Panama Canal. All in all, it is clear that environment, whether the accident of his birth and growth in the Salinas Valley of California or his own selection of various laboring jobs, figures largely in the source material of Steinbeck's writings.

YEARS OF SOCIAL UNREST: It should be pointed out that Steinbeck's long residence in the Salinas Valley covered years of both regional and national unrest, changes which he observed and later utilized especially in his three most sociologically oriented novels: *In Dubious Battle* (1936), *Of Mice and Men* (1937), and *The Grapes of Wrath* (1939). The economic structure of the Salinas Valley itself altered, as small farms were replaced by larger ones and the financial picture enlarged to include corporations, large investments and amassing fortunes. As the gap lengthened between the little man working for the big man, discontent also increased, with unemployment and threatened strikes. It was all part of the generalized national situation which culminated in the stock market crash of 1929 and the depression period following. Steinbeck's first published novel, in fact (*Cup of Gold*), appeared two months after the crash. The next few years were especially lean ones for him, as they were for many Americans, although he married, continued writing partly through a small subsidy and house provided by his father, and made the acquaintance of a man who was to exert significant influence on his life for many years to come—Edward Ricketts.

STEINBECK'S FRIENDSHIP WITH ED RICKETTS: A word or two should be said about Steinbeck's friendship with Ed Ricketts, the marine biologist, which lasted from their acquaintance in the 1930's until Ricketts' death in 1948. Ricketts had a commercial laboratory specializing in marine invertebrates in Pacific Grove, California; and he, along with his profession, apparently elicited and guided Steinbeck's similar interests in marine biology to specific expression in a work called the *Sea of Cortez* (a record of their joint expedition to the Gulf of California) and toward the general "biological view of life" which pervades much of his writing. (Steinbeck pays especial tribute to his friend in the preface to *Sea of Cortez,* in "About Ed Ricketts".) Ricketts is clearly the figure behind some of Steinbeck's most sympathetic portrayals of character

(Dr. Phillips in "The Snake," Doc Burton of *In Dubious Battle,* Doc of *Cannery Row* and *Sweet Thursday*), presumably the spokesman for ideas the two men jointly held. Theirs was an intellectual relationship in which Steinbeck was able to air his views and to arrive at some of his central artistic tenets.

STEINBECK IN RECENT YEARS: Steinbeck has of course written prolifically and variously over the years since 1929. One of the major changes in his life, however, has been his shift of residence from California to New York in 1950, where he has since lived. (The decision is often attributed in part to his deep sense of personal loss at the death of his friend Ricketts in 1948.) Significantly, a recent work, *The Winter of Our Discontent* (1961), was set in New England. Also, an account of travels throughout the United States, published in 1962 as *Travels with Charley,* seems to reflect the author's urge in the 1960's toward a revitalization of his creative powers. Steinbeck was awarded the Nobel Prize for Literature in 1962, honored, according to the official wording, for his "realistic and imaginative writings, distinguished as they are by a sympathetic humor and a social perception." He continues to comment, through fiction and non-fiction, in current periodicals.

LIST OF MAJOR WORKS: Steinbeck's major works to date are as follows: *Cup of Gold,* 1929; *The Pastures of Heaven,* 1932; *To a God Unknown,* 1933; *Tortilla Flat,* 1935; *In Dubious Battle,* 1936; *The Red Pony,* 1937; *Of Mice and Men,* 1937; *The Long Valley,* 1938; *The Grapes of Wrath,* 1939; *Sea of Cortez,* 1941; *Bombs Away,* 1942; *The Moon Is Down,* 1942 (this work and *Of Mice and Men* also appear as plays); *Cannery Row,* 1945; *The Pearl,* 1947; *The Wayward Bus,* 1947; *East of Eden,* 1952; *Sweet Thursday,* 1954; *The Short Reign of Pippin IV,* 1957; *The Winter of Our Discontent,* 1961; *Travels with Charley,* 1962. (It should be noted that it is a second version of the Sea of Cortez expedition, published as *The Log from the Sea of Cortez,* 1951, and containing only the "Introduction" and "Narrative" from *Sea of Cortez,* which contains the memorial sketch of Ed Ricketts referred to above.)

STEINBECK'S MAJOR ATTITUDES AND THEMES, BIOLOGICAL THEORY OF MAN: Since certain attitudes and themes on the part of Steinbeck are commonly referred to by critics and recur in most of his writings, including *The Grapes of Wrath,* it is worthwhile to review them briefly before turning to a detailed consideration of the novel at hand. One such attitude has been referred to above as a biological view of man, developed at least in part through Steinbeck's close association with his friend the marine biologist. A simple statement of this view is sufficient for the present (saving the contradictions of critics for a discussion under "Critical Summary"). Steinbeck relates human beings—his fictional characters—to plants and animals; he seems to see analogies of man in nature, in a manner not so unlike the American Transcendentalists as represented especially by Emerson and Thoreau, who maintained a mystical reverence for all forms of natural life. His emphasis of course is on the natural over the supernatural; but nature in its phenomena and cycles offers even more than simple analogy, Steinbeck seems to suggest. It offers an almost spiritual comfort and encourages an earth-founded optimism.

PHILOSOPHY OF THE NON-TELEOLOGICAL: The above term—non-teleological—is often linked with Steinbeck's biological view of man. Steinbeck himself has referred to this "philosophy"—perhaps because of his constantly refreshing urge to communicate to readers by making ideas as concrete as possible—as "is" thinking. As certain critics have explained it, "is" thinking represents "Steinbeck's own attempt to make the technical term *non-teleological* more meaningful to his readers. Broadly what Steinbeck means is a way of thinking about life that, by concerning itself with what *is,* not with the questions of *why* or *what should be,* avoids the false judgments and exclusions of a squeamish and snobbish morality and achieves love of life through acceptance." (E. W. Tedlock, Jr. and C. V. Wicker, *Steinbeck and his Critics.*) Such an attitude is very much in the spirit of what the famous American psychologist and philosopher William James termed "pragmatism," for pragmatism suggests that a man's thought and his action go hand in hand and requires that men reason about and judge events as they are experiencing them, instead of applying facilely to their experiences preconceived "why's" and "what should be's." "Is" thinking, or pragmatic thinking, then, recognizes that theoretical or abstract thought does not always fit reality, the way life really happens: to form such a way of thinking into a kind of philosophy, as Steinbeck seems to do, is to express one's belief in a human world of realizable goals rather than a dream world of impossible ideals.

STEINBECK'S SOCIAL CONSCIOUSNESS: Although it is perhaps unfortunate for Steinbeck's total literary reputation that the first three of his novels which received serious critical attention were sociologically oriented, since this has caused many critics to read social criticism forcibly into all his works, it is nevertheless certainly true that social consciousness represents a basic element in his writings, and especially in *In Dubious Battle* (1936), *Of Mice and Men* (1937), and *The Grapes of Wrath* (1939), all of which were post-depression novels and dealt with proletarian matter. The first-mentioned novel is concerned with specific social problems of the period —violence, particularly of strikes and strikebreaking, and the ineffectuality of both "left" and "right," politically speaking, in bringing about more humane conditions and equitable solutions to labor conflicts. The second novel is more involved with men—little men—and their struggles than with generalized social problems. Of this story, about a feeble-minded character Lennie and his friend George who dream of owning a farm in California, Steinbeck wrote that he was dealing with "the earth longings of a Lennie who was not to represent insanity at all but the inarticulate and powerful yearning of all men." At another time he declared that *Of Mice and Men* was "a study of the dreams and pleasures of everyone in the world," an indication of the continuing emphasis in his writings on individual man and his strivings rather than stark social criticism. *The Grapes of Wrath,* to be treated below, is of course his epic masterpiece of social consciousness in its picture of helpless people crushed by drought and depression. Even here, though, as in all his works to follow, Steinbeck's focus is upon man, the nature of man and his successes and failures, rather than upon the mere detached picture of an indifferent society (in contrast, for example, to some of Steinbeck's immediate forerunners in American fiction, such as Frank Norris and Theodore Dreiser, who depicted man simply as a wisp in the wind of giant American industrialism and stampeding capitalism).

DREAM AND REALITY, A FANTASY WORLD: There is an element in Steinbeck's fiction which belongs more to a fantasy or dream world than it does to the real everyday world: sometimes this element manifests itself in the author's choice of protagonists from among the feeble-minded, the castoffs of society, the antisocial; in other instances it is seen in his descriptions, which often open chapters, and conjure up a dreamlike atmosphere (this descriptive quality is especially evident in *Tortilla Flat, Cannery Row* and *Sweet Thursday*). Steinbeck's choice of central characters, in particular, has caused much controversy among critics as to his intentions and the successful realization of them. He has been accused of "glorifying idiocy," (for example, in Lennie, *Of Mice and Men*), or of "deifying the drunk, canonizing the castoff"—the major figures in *Cannery Row*, for instance, by his own stipulation, are society's "no-goods and blots-on-the-town and bums." Similarly, Danny and his friends (in *Tortilla Flat*) live what by ordinary standards is certainly an unreal existence, surviving more through chance than any calculation and "experiencing" in a most random way. Or, the characters in *The Wayward Bus* seem selected by the author more for some separate point he wishes to probe about each of them than for the likelihood that they could have in reality been thrust together for the rambling bus ride.

We have seen that of Lennie the halfwit (*Of Mice and Men*) Steinbeck stated he was to represent "the inarticulate and powerful yearning of all men. . . . the dreams and pleasures of everyone in the world." It is likewise clear from Steinbeck's numerous statements on the book *Tortilla Flat*, which is episodic (that is, it seems to be a series of episodes strung together, often by dreamlike descriptions), that he intended it to be a kind of modern Arthurian cycle, a story of 20th century knights of the Round Table, although related in a mock-epic or humorous tone. (The author has spoken, for example, as late as 1957—*Tortilla Flat* is dated 1935—of his continuing interest in Sir Thomas Malory's *Le Morte d'Arthur* and his desire to travel to England to study the manuscript and discuss it with an Arthurian scholar.) Similar objectives outside realistic narrative along the lines of allegorical symbolic meanings, can be detected in, say, *The Wayward Bus*, which Steinbeck concludes with an epigraph quoting from a well-known Medieval "morality" play called *Everyman*, a drama which chronicled (somewhat like the familiar *Pilgrim's Progress* of John Bunyan) the cycle of *every man's* life from birth to death. These few examples indicate that however critics may judge his efforts or however his goals are actually realized, in much of his work Steinbeck is striving beyond realistic narrative or mere social protest, attempting to chronicle, in near-epic form, the struggles of individual men. Those critics who have gotten especially close to Steinbeck's work in all its stages (for example, Peter Lisca, E. W. Tedlock, Jr., C. V. Wicker, Warren French) attest to the comprehensiveness and complexity of his plan and approach for each novel.

A final example of Steinbeck's concern with good and evil in human experience and with the possibility of choice may be cited. In the dedication to his novel *East of Eden* he indicated that he had struggled considerably with the problem of good and evil in human existence; he chose to symbolize this struggle by placing the Hebrew world *timshel* on the cover, which is interpreted "thou mayest," and stands for the question of ethical choice in the novel. In both the American Standard Bible and the King James version the expression reads "Do thou rule over him," or "and thou shalt rule over him"; but as one of the characters in the book points out, "Don't you see?' he cried. 'The American Standard translation *orders* men to triumph over sin. But the Hebrew word, the word *timshel*—

"Thou mayest"—that gives a choice. It might be the most important word in the world.' "

Going back for a moment to that world which Steinbeck evokes through vivid descriptions, which often prelude or are interspersed among his dialogues and actions, we recall that he fixed upon visual sensations of nature (the hopping sparrows) or feelings elicited by nature's events (the birth of a colt) as significant biographical material. Before beginning "The Red Pony" (which is seen by most commentators to be very close to Steinbeck's own boyhood), he remarked: "I want to recreate a child's world, not of fairies and giants but of colors more clear than they are to adults, of tastes more sharp and of queer heartbreaking feelings that overwhelm children in a moment. I want to put down the way 'afternoon felt'—and the feeling about a bird that sang in a tree in the evening." It would seem then that in his fantasy or dream worlds, in his "unreal" characters, all focused on the sphere of nature, he is striving to reproduce a childlike state of existence, from which can be derived philosophical, even mystical implications. This has led his more serious critics to describe him as "the first significant novelist to begin to build a mystical religion upon a naturalistic base."

STEINBECK'S ATTITUDES TOWARD POPULARITY AND CRITICISM: Because Steinbeck is a contemporary writer whose comments may appear regularly on the printed page—and because some of his past remarks, or defenses, regarding his own work and the critics reveal a sense of the ironic and the absurd which is also a key to some of his fictional effects—it is worth devoting a word or two here to his attitudes toward popular success and critics. At least up until the more recent years of his residence in the East, Steinbeck has been noted for his resistance to invasions upon his personal life as well as for his refusal to respond to the baiting of critics who choose to interpret him in flatly contradicting terms. Asked, for example, in 1951 by the American Humanist Association to classify himself in one of six categories of humanism, he replied that his approach to philosophy was "on tiptoe ready to run at the

first growl"; he further disclaimed on that occasion an awareness of what his own philosophy was about, even questioning
whether or not he had a philosophy. Another example of
"Steinbeck and the Critics" is his recent reply to the invita-
tion of *The Colorado Quarterly* to comment on a critical controversy raging between Bernard Bowron and Warren G.
French over the merits of *The Grapes of Wrath;* in "A Letter
on Criticism" Steinbeck smoothly refused to become involved,
even on the side of his defender, Warren G. French, and in-
dulged in some biting wit against criticism in general, remark-
ing, for example, that he is not against criticism so long as it
is understood to be "a kind of ill tempered parlour game in
which nobody gets kissed." He added wrily that "recently a
critic proved by parallel passages that I had taken my whole
philosophy from a 17th century Frenchman of whom I had
never heard." His real point—or most worthwhile point—in
the letter, perhaps, is that "the writing of books is a lonely and
difficult job. . . ."

It does appear that, for whatever reasons, Steinbeck maintains
a deep-seated mistrust of literary critics, at least when they
seem to him to stand for intellectualism gone on a sterile ram-
page; it would certainly seem that such expressions as the letter
quoted above display a hostility represented by a kind of Tru-
manesque hauling-off at the critics with sweeping generalizations ("In less criticismal terms, I think it is a bunch of crap")
which are hardly less childish than the pedantic pickings of
cloistered scholars. It is interesting to note that at the same
time Steinbeck, especially from about 1930 to 1945, had a
great fear of popular success, or at least of being labelled as
a "regional" writer or a "primitive" writer or a "humorist."
The partial result of this wish to avoid popular success may have
been his shifting about from social protest to pastoral-like
tales to allegorical/symbolic devices. In recent years, however,
the writer has seemed more friendly or tolerant toward the
reading public and his critics.

THE GRAPES OF WRATH, BACKGROUND: The background upon which John Steinbeck drew to write *The Grapes*

of Wrath is impressive. We have already reviewed the record of his youth among the small farms in the Salinas Valley of California, as well as his early, varied employment and travel experiences. His novel *In Dubious Battle* (1936) called attention to him as social critic and spokesman for California migrants. During that same year he wrote a series of articles for the *San Francisco News* depicting the miserable conditions of the migrant camps near Salinas and Bakersfield. In the fall of 1937, after working in New York on the project of turning *Of Mice and Men* into a play, he bought a car and drove to Oklahoma to join the migrant workers, traveling with them, camping alongside the road with them, accompanying them to California. At one point he was so disturbed by their impoverished conditions that he wanted to accept a Hollywood contract of $1000 a week for six weeks, on *Of Mice and Men,* in order to give two dollars apiece to 3000 migrant workers. (His agent flew to the coast to talk him out of it.) On another occasion he refused to go into the field with a photographer and observe the migrants for a paid article for *Life* magazine, saying "I'm sorry but I simply can't make money on these people . . . the suffering is too great for me to cash in on it." Steinbeck's experiences with the migrant workers have been related in two ways, one graphic and reportorial, the other artistic and creative. In 1938 he recorded these experiences in what has been until recently a little-known and out-of-print pamphlet titled *Their Blood Is Strong,* published by an organization in California called the Lubin Society which had been formed, with the backing of the governor at that time (Culbert L. Olson) and other political and social leaders, "to educate public opinion to an understanding of the problems of the working farmer and the condition of agricultural laborers, and the need of them both for progressive organization to better their conditions." It should be emphasized that there is a vast distinction to be made between Steinbeck's newspaper report of the migrants' plight and his now-famous novel *The Grapes of Wrath;* there is some value in knowing, however, the actual background of experience from which the author worked on his novel, just as there is interesting "extra" information contained in the pamphlet, such as Steinbeck's ideas of what might have been immediate solutions to the migrants' problems.

THE GRAPES OF WRATH, RECEPTION: The startled, even outraged reception of *The Grapes of Wrath* at its publication in 1939 is fairly well-known. As Peter Lisca describes it, *"The Grapes of Wrath* was a phenomenon on the scale of a national event. It was publicly banned and burned by citizens; it was debated on national radio hook-ups; but above all it was read. Those who didn't read it saw it as a motion picture. It brought Steinbeck the Pulitzer prize and got him elected to the National Institute of Arts and Letters."* In short, the book was timely and authentic, and it stepped on a lot of toes, particularly regional ones in Oklahoma and California. (One recalls an earlier, if less vehement and far-reaching, protest of the citizens of Monterey, California against Steinbeck's *Tortilla Flat;* fearful that the novel would damage their tourist trade, they exclaimed that Monterey wasn't like that, full of "no-goods and bums.") Lisca records one isolated response which especially pleased Steinbeck: "A group of migrant laborers sent him a patchwork dog sewn from pieces of their shirt-tails and dresses and bearing around its neck a tag with the inscription 'Migrant John.'"

There is no mistaking the fact that in absorbing his material for the novel firsthand, Steinbeck was practicing what we have referred to as his pragmatic view of life, life as it, in this case unfortunately, "is." At the same time he was reminding a good many hitherto rather silent Americans of the "why's" and the "what should be's"—hence the troubled and hugely publicized reaction. The honest attempt of one critic to assess this reaction to the novel, soon after its publication, in 1944, is worth entering here, especially since it implies part of the modern social validity of the novel. Martin Staples Shockley concluded that "properly speaking, *The Grapes of Wrath* is not a regional novel; but it has regional significance; it raises regional problems. Economic collapse, farm tenantry, migratory labor are not regional problems; they are national or international in scope, and can never be solved through state or regional action." Artistically speaking, Steinbeck himself has perhaps best expressed how he hoped to metamorphose social fact into art in the novel; he says that he was "simply listening to men talk and watching them act, hoping that the projection of the microcosm will define the outlines of the macrocosm." In other words, Steinbeck is making here almost a general statement of the theory of art: the artist selects and puts together the specific and concrete of men's lives in the hope that from the total picture, universal truths will emerge. Also, in his pronouncement, Steinbeck has put his finger on what is the continuing greatness, down to the present day of readers, of *The Grapes of Wrath*.

THE GRAPES OF WRATH: PLOT ANALYSIS

CHAPTERS 1, 2 AND 3

The first chapter of the novel establishes a situation and an atmosphere, from which will emerge the people and the happenings: the devastation of the drought to the land is described in detail, along with the effect it has had upon the people and their lives. They huddle in their houses, or protect themselves from the seeping dust when they go out, for the wind viciously raises the dust from time to time. The women and children watch the men to see if they are going to stand up under the strain; for the moment they do. Into this ominous atmosphere walks Tom Joad, in the second chapter, hitchhiking home from prison in cheap, new clothes, released on parole after serving four years of a seven-year sentence for homicide. Although the red transport truck carries a sticker stating "No Riders," Tom talks the driver into a ride when he emerges from the restaurant, because the driver wants to be considered a "good guy," one who can't be kicked around by "rich bastards." As the two men roar down the road together, the truckdriver confides his ambitions to get ahead and, none too subtly, elicits the facts of Tom's immediate past. As they part, he wishes Tom luck. Chapter Three carefully details the progress of a horny beaked land turtle up onto the highway embankment and along the road. A woman driving a sedan swerves to avoid hitting the turtle, but the driver of the truck which has just put down Tom Joad tries, unsuccessfully, to hit it.

COMMENT

DESCRIPTION OF THE DROUGHT: The opening paragraph of the novel—indeed, the entire first chapter—is an exquisitely worked out prelude to the whole action and outcome of *The Grapes of Wrath*. (The passage of course has become rather well-known as a classic of prose style, and is often anthologized.) Beginning with "to the red country and part of the gray country of Oklahoma, the last rains came gently, and they did not cut the scarred earth," the author chronicles in the initial paragraph, chiefly through use of colors, the progressive destruction of the drought: "the surface of the earth crusted, a thin hard crust, and as the sky became pale, so the earth became pale, pink in the red country and white in the gray country." The fact that the color of a whole countryside could be changed by burning sun and lack of rain has an overwhelming effect on the reader: red turns to pink, gray to white, green to brown; the ploughed earth becomes thin hard crust. It is a growth cycle grimly reversed.

The oppressive atmosphere builds with the dawn which depressingly brings no day, and with the picture of men and women huddled in their houses. "The dawn came, but no day. In the gray sky a red sun apeared, a dim red circle that gave a little light, like dusk; and as that day advanced, the dusk slipped back toward darkness, and the wind cried and whimpered over the fallen corn." In this pathetic and poetic paragraph, the sun and the wind seem as much like actors in some silent drama as the huddled people who lie and wait for the dust to settle. Nor does the concluding passage of Chapter One relieve the heavy mood established by Steinbeck: the people come out of their houses tense and watchful, and there is grim decision in the air, hanging on the question of whether or not the men will "break." "The women studied the men's faces secretly, for the corn could go, as long as something else remained." And for the moment the tension is dissipated. "After a while the faces of the watching men lost their bemused perplexity and became hard and angry and resistant. Then the women knew that they were safe and that there was no break. . . . Women and children knew deep in themselves that no misfortune was too great to bear if their men were whole. The women went into the houses to their work, and the children began to play, but cautiously at first. As the day went forward the sun became less red. It flared down on the dust-blanketed land. The men sat in the doorways of their houses; their hands

were busy with sticks and little rocks. The men sat still—
thinking—figuring."

**WHAT IS ESTABLISHED IN CHAPTER ONE, A SITUATION OF
EPIC PROPORTIONS:**   The effect of the graphic, even an-
guished, description of the physical state of things and, by implication, the mental state, is to make the reader aware of
pending crises as yet unseen and whole worlds or ways of life
hanging in the balance. We note that no particular people
have yet been introduced—i.e., the Joads—and the rather
generalized men, women and children who stand about bewildered in the dust seem almost to be pantomimists in some
ageless and universal drama. Immediately, and wisely from a
literary point of view, the author is going to particularize the
action into a crisis for the Joad family; but the first lines of
the novel suggest significantly that the problem of survival is
timeless, elemental, and common to all mankind.

Another theme, related to the one of survival, is established
here, in the threatened loss of human dignity. The immediate
crisis is essentially economic but is seen as closely related to
loss of morale: the primary concern of the women is that their
men remain whole, that they give battle to adverse circum-
stance. The twin themes of economic and moral decline are of
course integral to the novel; they will clash throughout with
the lingering impetus to survive. (One of the things which
Steinbeck was most vigorously outspoken about in the newspaper articles published as the pamphlet *Their Blood Is Strong*
was this slow but steady demoralization and loss of personal
esteem in the men, customarily regarded as heads of the family
unit. More recent commentators on the conditions of poverty
—for instance, Michael Harrington in *The Other America*—
also cite the deep psychological damage to the man which
often begins with loss of the means of livelihood, whether
through losing his job and being unable to get another one or,
here, having his land destroyed or much diminished in value
and ultimately being dispossessed of it.)

THE DUST AS A SYMBOL: The word *dust* is repeated 27 times in Chapter One, and such repetition reinforces one of the themes—or in fact the twin themes mentioned above: economic decline which will accumulate into disaster, and deteriorating morale which will at length split up the family unit. For the dust is all-pervading, and can be said to symbolize the downward-settling fortunes of the Joad family, and of all the people caught up in its destructive swirl. It is out of the land that the novel's action develops, and the land has turned to dust. Note the following examples of the author's utilization of every possible visual and aural (the same consonant or vowel sounds) effect with *dust*, along with the invariable association of dust with what is dying or dead: "the earth dusted down in dry little streams"; "every moving thing lifted the dust into the air"; "the dust from the roads fluffed up"; "the sky was darkened by the mixing dust, and the wind felt over the earth, loosened the dust, and carried it away"; "the stars could not pierce the dust to get down." Other examples of similar sounds are *crust, fluffed, brushed, muffled*. The wind becomes an agent of the demonic dust, almost personified as it "feels" over the earth, assisting the dust to dominate the other natural elements of air, sky, sun, stars. The women must battle the dust on their windows and door sills, the children are obliged to play in it—"they drew careful lines in the dust with their toes"—and the endurance of the men is tested as they face the "ruined corn, drying fast now, only a little green showing through the film of dust."

INTERCHAPTERS IN *THE GRAPES OF WRATH*:   Chapter One introduces Steinbeck's use of what are usually termed "interchapters" in this novel. There are 16 interchapters altogether, spanning about 100 pages. Most of these interchapters furnish social background which illuminates the actions of the Joad family (i.e., the conflict between the banks and the farmers; buying a car; selling household goods); a few provide historical or other information (the history of migrant labor; land ownership in California; Highway #66). The description of the drought and later, of the rains, of course records dynamic natural phenomena out of which socio-economic changes are forcibly wrought. The interchapters are always interwoven with chapters before and after, in a manner which will be explained in the commentaries following.

AN ACTUAL ACCOUNT OF DROUGHT IN OKLAHOMA:

For those who have never visited the dust bowl or experienced a dust storm it will be of interest to quote briefly from one of a series of "Letters from the Dust Bowl" written during the summer of 1935 by Mrs. Caroline A. Henderson and subsequently published in *The Atlantic Monthly*. Mrs. Henderson speaks first to her friend "Evelyn" of the startling "transition from rain-soaked eastern Kansas with its green pastures, luxuriant foliage, abundance of flowers, and promise of a generous harvest, to the dust-covered desolation of No Man's Land." She describes their present conditions: "Wearing our shade hats, with handkerchiefs tied over our faces and Vaseline in our nostrils, we have been trying to rescue our home from the accumulations of wind-blown dust which penetrates wherever air can go. It is an almost hopeless task, for there is rarely a day when at some time the dust clouds do not roll over. 'Visibility' approaches zero and everything is covered again with a siltlike deposit which may vary in depth from a film to actual ripples on the kitchen floor. I keep oiled cloths on the window sills and between the upper and lower sashes." Mrs. Henderson also remarks with sympathy, incidentally, on the number of families who have been forced out of the area, describing the "pitiful reminders of broken hopes and apparently wasted effort" she encountered driving through the countryside. "Little abandoned homes where people had drilled deep wells for the precious water, had set trees and vines, built reservoirs, and fenced in gardens—with everything now walled in or half buried by banks of drifted soil—told a painful story of loss and disappointment." (This series of letters, and other invaluable and interesting background to *The Grapes of Wrath*, can be found in Warren French, *A Companion to The Grapes of Wrath*, New York, 1963. French, a biographer of John Steinbeck, divides his small and useful volume into Background, Reception and Reputation of the novel, and provides answers to such intriguing questions as What Was the Dust Bowl? Who Were the "Okies"? How Was The Grapes of

Wrath Received at Home? Was The Grapes of Wrath Answered? Is the Movie Like the Book? etc.)

CHAPTER THREE, THE TURTLE: When total chapters, even short ones, are devoted to turtles, we are obliged to look for significance. Just as Chapter One was a masterpiece of poetic, almost biblical, evocation, so Chapter Three—an interchapter —is a masterly specimen of scientific-like observation of the turtle's minutest movements. First of all, then, the chapter has value as technique, as excellent realistic description. It is clear, though, that the activities of the turtle are not to be discounted; and indeed, he reappears in the next chapter, picked up by Tom Joad and commented upon by that character who is of such philosophical importance in the novel, Jim Casy. (The reappearance of the turtle in Chapter Four is in fact a simple instance of the way Steinbeck interlocks chapters and interchapters, as suggested above. Such repetitions, in other words, are ways of unifying a novel, and are especially meaningful if the recurring thing or idea is of thematic or symbolic value.)

If we examine the brief adventure of the turtle, we find that he covers the grass, "leaving a beaten trail behind him." Then he confronts a hill—the highway embankment—and methodically negotiates it to the flat and easier going surface of the highway, having mastered—straining, slipping, lifting—the 4-inch concrete wall which borders the road, no mean achievement, we are made to see through the detail, for a turtle. And we note that the turtle has crushed a red ant in his climb. He is also dragging along with his front legs a head of wild oats— the "beards" mentioned in the first paragraph, which contain seeds. The rest of his adventure is comprised of crossing the highway, where a woman swerves (with some danger to herself—"the wheels screamed . . . two wheels lifted for a moment and then settled") to avoid hitting him but the truck driver who has just dropped off Tom Joad (which is a unifying link with the foregoing chapter) tries to smash him. Another matter worth noting is that the turtle is emphasized in his ancient, enduring, almost primeval qualities: "high-domed shell . . .

hard legs and yellow-nailed feet . . . horny beak . . . old humorous frowning eyes."

The turtle, of course, stands for survival, for the mysterious and instinctive life force which prompts him to begin over again each time, despite setbacks, his laborious progress and which likewise will impel the Joads onward to California. The turtle crushes a red ant which gets in the way of his armored shell, and survives the truck driver's attempt to crush him. (And at this point we recall the aggressiveness of the driver: his delight in probing the secrets out of people; his desire to train his mind all the time, and to take some correspondence school courses; his yearning to "tell other guys to drive trucks." He is a man who intends, at least in a vague way—"just study a few easy lessons at home. I'm thinkin' of it"—to get ahead.) Similarly, the Joads will endure and overcome the obstacles to their journey to California. Even more significant to our understanding of the symbolic value of the turtle is the fact that when he had regained his upright position on the other side of the road, "the wild oat head fell out and three of the spearhead seeds stuck in the ground. And as the turtle crawled on down the embankment, its shell dragged dirt over the seeds." The turtle in his laborious progress yet perpetuates life, assists in the initiation of a new growth cycle. The important idea of rebirth in the analogy between the turtle and the Joads can be discussed more fully in our interpretation of the ending of the novel.

CHAPTERS 4, 5 AND 6

Young Tom Joad, having removed his uncomfortable shoes to pad in the dust, sights the familiar land turtle and picks it up. Under the shade of the tree he heads for to seek relief from the boiling sun he discovers a figure from his past, the preacher Jim Casy. (It is the preacher in fact that he has referred to a few minutes ago as a man who knew big words; again, unity is strengthened by the link through "preacher" between Chapters 2 and 4, especially since Casy will figure largely in the action of the novel.) But Jim Casy, always a thinker, has now thought himself out of being a preacher. He has decided that in good conscience he can no longer preach, although he asserts "I got the call to lead the people, an' no place to lead 'em." He loves people, he says, but he has lost faith in religion. Together Casy and Tom come upon the deserted Joad homestead, the reasons for its desertion having been eloquently explained in the previous interchapter, which traces the developments by which the land was taken out of the hands of the tenants by the owners, or rather by the twin inanimate monsters of the tractor and the bank. Tom and the reverend are at a loss to discover why the Joads have left, without any word to their absent son, however, until a former neighbor, Muley Graves, happens along and relates to them what has been happening. Tom hears how his grampa and pa put up a good fight before eviction, but that the events "took somepin outa Tom." Muley's existence has been warped into strangeness by the changes, too: all his folks have gone on to California, but he could not bring himself to leave the land; he wanders around sleeping and eating in a fugitive fashion— " 'like a damn ol' graveyard ghos,' " he says. On this occasion he shares with the other two men his trappings of the day—two cottontails and a jackrabbit—and there is some philosophizing around the fire until the three are forced to hide by authorities who have seen their light and come to check on "trespassers." They sleep that night in the bottom of the dried-up gulch.

COMMENT

JIM CASY, PHILOSOPHER, PROPHET: From the moment Jim Casy reveals that he isn't preaching anymore—"Ain't got the call no more. Got a lot of sinful idears—but they seem kinda sensible"—there is the implication, soon borne out, that he is to function as some sort of spokesman for reorientations, for new ideas. As he talks on it becomes clear that he has been and is experiencing a sort of spiritual rebirth; and in fact the theme of rebirth, suggested in the seeds dropped by the turtle, is now picked up by Casy. Steinbeck dwells for a moment upon the habits of the turtle, always "goin' someplace," to implant the idea of Jim Casy's future leadership. Casy points out, "Nobody can't keep a turtle though. They work at it and work at it, and at last one day they get out and away they go—off somewheres. [This syndrome is demonstrated by the turtle, in Chapter Six.] It's like me. I wouldn' take the good ol' gospel that was just layin' there to my hand. I got to be pickin' at it an' workin' at it until I got it all tore down. Here I got the sperit sometimes an' nothin' to preach about. I got the call to lead the people, an' no place to lead 'em." Jim is so bothered by this thought that he applies it again to the passing dog that ignores Tom's friendly whistle. " 'Goin' someplace," he repeated 'That's right, he's goin' someplace. Me—I don't know where I'm goin'." Jim is clearly searching for a place, a new and worthwhile function.

The subject of Jim's reorientation is brought up again; for he still claims to have "the sperit" but he has been forced to examine himself on a number of matters connected with religion as he has formerly practiced it. For one thing, his sensuality has disturbed him; he has not, for example, been able to fit sex and his relish for it—particularly after riproaring revivalist meetings with the girls from his audience—into the context of his religion. But he ponders, "Maybe it ain't a sin. Maybe it's just the way folks is. Maybe we been whippin' the hell out of ourselves for nothin'." And he wrestles with definitions of sin and virtue. It is the nature of "sperit" which most puzzles and consumes him, though; at one point he asserts (significantly, for Jim Casy is being shaped for the reader into a humanist), "It's love. I love people so much I'm fit to bust, sometimes." But it is in the question of "Jesus" that his supposed heresy rests. "An' I says, 'Don't you love Jesus?' Well, I thought an' thought, an' finally I says, 'No, I don't know nobody name' Jesus. I know a bunch of stories, but I only love people." In fact—and this is the core of the philosophical stand which Jim Casy will take throughout the novel—he has "figgered" a lot about "the Holy Sperit and the Jesus road. I figgered, 'Why do we got to hang it on God or Jesus? Maybe,' I figgered, 'maybe it's all men an' all women we love; maybe that's the Holy Sperit—the human sperit—the whole shebang. Maybe all men got one big soul ever'body's a part of.'" Jim's revelation, which he knows "deep down" is true, actually has a rather fancy name in the history of American philosophical thought: he has just announced his intuition of the "Transcendental Oversoul," but in somewhat earthier terms than his unseen mentor and chief proponent of the concept, Ralph Waldo Emerson, ever spoke.

In short, one of the strands of the social philosophy which Steinbeck develops during the novel can be traced to American Transcendentalism, with its concept of the Oversoul—"one big soul ever'body's a part of"—with its faith in the common man and in self-reliance. The philosophy will be most often spoken by the "prophet," Jim Casy, and it will be acted out by the Joads and their fellows. For Jim's new calling, of course, will be to follow the trek westward, since he decides that these people "gonna need help no preachin' can give 'em. Hope of heaven when their lives ain't lived? Holy Sperit when their own sperit is downcast an' sad? They gonna need help. They got to live before they can afford to die." And in this statement Jim places a most ironic finger on the inadequate, unrealistic and even hypocritical premises of his religion as he has come to view it: he can no longer continue his pat offers of future paradise or his hair-raising portrayals of hellfire and brimstone before the present and nauseatingly real wretchedness of his people.

NOTES OF PATHOS: The ideas of humanism, love of mankind introduced in these chapters are reinforced by notes of
pathos here and there. Tom Joad, for example, has picked up
the turtle to take to his little brother, because he knows "kids
like turtles." He retrieves the turtle once, in fact, before at
last releasing it when he finds his family departed, explaining,
"I ain't got no present for the kids. . . . Nothin' but this ol'
turtle." Also, there is a pathetically human absurdity in Granma's Christmas card to Tom in prison, which caused his cell-
mates to call him "Jesus meek"; as Tom points out, again
demonstrating his awareness of the human condition (evidence
that he, like Jim Casy, may eventually undergo some sort of
education and conversion during the novel): "I guess Granma
never read it. Prob'ly got it from a drummer an' picked out
the one with the mos' shiny stuff on it. . . . Granma never
meant it funny; she jus' figgered it was so purty she wouldn't
bother to read it. She lost her glasses the year I went up.
Maybe she never did find 'em." Tom shows compassion here,
just as he does a few pages later when he mentions his hope
to have found his sister Rose of Sharon helping take some of
the burden of work from his mother.

Also, the theme of human dignity—preservation or loss of it—
again arises in these chapters. The dispossessed and bewildered
Muley Graves is a pathetic figure. He insists he was unable to
accompany his folks to California—"Somepin jus' wouldn' let
me"—yet he is only half-alive, like an old graveyard ghost,
and when asked to come along the next day to Uncle John's
and perhaps westward he replies, "Huh? No. I don't go no
place, an' I don't leave no place." And at night there is his
womblike withdrawal into his protective cave: "Muley pulled
at the covering brush and crawled into his cave. 'I like it in
here,' he called. 'I feel like nobody can come at me.' In spite
of his companions' protests to the contrary, Muley is one who
has indeed become a little "touched" by the upheavals which
have occurred. Old Tom's self-esteem has suffered, too—"it
took somepin outa Tom"—although young Tom resists hiding
in the cotton from the deputy sheriff, exclaiming "Jesus, I hate
to get pushed around!" Perhaps the tenant in Chapter 5

assesses pretty well the deep-rooted attachment of these men, especially the older ones, to their land, and the trauma of being uprooted: "Funny thing how it is. If a man owns a little property, that property is him, it's part of him, and it's like him. If he owns property only so he can walk on it and handle it and be sad when it isn't doing well, and feel fine when the rain falls on it, that property is him, and some way he's bigger because he owns it."

INTERCHAPTER FIVE, FORECLOSURES: Although it is a dialogue between the owners of the land, or their representatives, and the tenants, this interchapter presents groups—the classes involved in the conflict, we might say—rather than particular people such as the Joads. Such a presentation emphasizes the far-reaching effect of the changes wrought by bank foreclosures and tractors: the reader perceives a panoramic mass of dispossessed people just as he had a panoramic vision of the dust in Chapter 1. And, of course, Steinbeck has chosen here to contrast heavily the humaneness of the tenants and their attachment to the land with the inhuman remoteness of the banks and inanimate monstrosity of the tractors, including their gloved and goggled drivers, regarded by the farmers as traitors to the land and to their own folks. Of the tractor driver—"Joe Davis's boy"—it is said that the "monster" in the background—bank, agency, company—had "goggled his mind, muzzled his speech, goggled his perception, muzzled his protest." The chapter provides social background for the narrative in the sense that it is the foreclosures, of course, which force the emigration.

CHAPTERS 7, 8 AND 9

It is a depressing prospect, for the unwilling emigrants at least—"in the towns, on the edges of the towns, in fields, in vacant lots, the used-car yards, the wreckers' yards, the garages with blazoned signs"—the glaring image presented in Chapter 7 of the used car hustlers, most of them "outsiders" who have hurried into the country to capitalize on the dire necessities of these dispossessed. Meanwhile, in Chapter 8, Tom and Jim Casy make their way toward Uncle John's, whose sad life story is related, and the structure of the Joad family is bit by bit unfolded as young Tom is reunited first with his father—"at last he touched Tom, but touched him on the shoulder, timidly, and instantly took his hand away"—then his mother—"she moved toward him lithely, soundlessly in her bare feet, and her face was full of wonder"—then the rest of the family, all of whom have changed in his four years' absence: Rose of Sharon married and pregnant, Al a tom-catting 16-year-old, Ruthie a young lady of 12, Winfield still gauche. They all breakfast together energetically, after a curious and meditative grace by their former preacher. But the necessary prelude to the long trek westward is to strip themselves of all but the necessary implements of utensils, bedding, clothes. The interchapter 9 poignantly images the general scene: an $18 Sears Roebuck plow, a fine team of mules with braided manes and forelocks, a dirty rag doll, a book called Pilgrim's Progress—all to be sold disastrously cheap, or discarded. "How can we live without our lives? How will we know it's us without our past? No. Leave it. Burn it." And of course take the rifle: "Wouldn't go out naked of a rifle."

COMMENT

INTERCHAPTER 7, BUYING A USED CAR: The ironic picture here of the imported used car dealers' exploitation of the evicted tenants is an interesting instance of the variety of

Steinbeck's prose style. The sentence structure in this chapter has been referred to by one critic as "staccato"; it is an abrupt and blunt style which the author utilizes throughout the novel, from time to time, often to achieve the effect of harsh, mechanical facts of life which frustrate bewildered people like the Joads. "Used Cars, Good Used Cars. Cheap transportation, three trailers. '27 Ford, clean. Checked cars, guaranteed cars. Free radio. Car with 100 gallons of gas free. Come in and look. Used Cars. No overhead. . . . Old monsters with deep upholstery—you can cut her into a truck easy. Two-wheel trailers, axles rusty in the hard afternoon sun. Used Cars. Good Used Cars. Clean, runs good. Don't pump oil." The short running sentences suggest the hustling and pressuring of the salesmen, while the repetitions emphasize the depressing frequency with which such scenes were enacted. The fast pace also reminds us of how the tenant-buyer was out of his element in such a setting, at a disadvantage, too "nice" as the salesman points out: "Get 'em under obligation. Make 'em take up your time. Don't let 'em forget they're takin' your time. People are nice, mostly. They hate to put you out. Make 'em put you out, an' then sock it to 'em." And the man searching among the glittering machines for one which will get him to California asks himself, "How do you buy a car? What does it cost? Watch the children, now. I wonder how much for this one? We'll ask. It don't cost money to ask. We can ask, can't we?" (This style of writing, incidentally, is reminiscent of what is called the "newsreel technique" of John dos Passos, American contemporary to Steinbeck; in the staccato quality and the pattern of repetition there is also a hint of the poetry of Carl Sandburg.)

GROUP, OR UNIT, INSTEAD OF INDIVIDUAL, A THEME:
One of the positive themes of the novel is suggested in Chapter 8 (the "negative" themes are those of economic and moral decline—shattering of the family unit and deteriorating self-esteem), a theme which by the end has become social prophecy. While it is true that the Joads are at first bound together as a family—and this is the structure that Ma in particular is stubbornly determined to preserve, although she sees it disin-

tegrating around her (with the death of Grampa, the disappearance of Noah, etc.)—there is a glimpse in Chapter 8, again through the eyes of Ma, whose matriarchal position enables her to understand the psychological and therefore real force of separate persons banded together, of the protection and power which might come out of group action. She has perceived the ineffectiveness of any one small, scared and angry man against the present adverse circumstances: "Tommy, don't you go fightin' 'em alone," she declares passionately. "I got to thinkin' an' dreamin' an' wonderin'. They say there's a hun'erd thousand of us shoved out. If we was all mad the same way, Tommy—they wouldn't hunt nobody down . . ." Tom seems to understand this somewhat revolutionary notion of Ma's, because he immediately asks if "many folks feel that way?" It is a theme, the idea that survival might rest in group action, which will pick up more and more momentum in the ensuing chapters, first when the Wilsons and the Joads join forces for their common welfare, later in the almost idyllic (it turns out) sanity of the government camp (where "community organization," as we know it today in the fight on poverty, is in full and effective operation), and of course in the ultimate reorientation of Tom Joad from a kind of primitive individualism—"I climb fences when I got fences to climb"—to his faltering conviction of Jim Casy's "one big soul" and of a notion of "social welfare"—"all work together for our own thing"—to be realized, unfortunately, in Tom's time only through social warfare.

MA, JIM CASY, AND THE THEME OF LOVE: Jim Casy's not-so-amateur philosophy of love, linked with his theory of "one big soul," was mentioned in Chapter 4. And his philosophy is actually a combination of the Transcendental "Oversoul" explored by Emerson, based on intuition (which the ex-preacher would be likely to regard as revelation), and the ideas of mass democracy, love of all men, found in the poetry of Walt Whitman (we can look upon the Whitmanesque tone in fact as the second strand of Steinbeck's "philosophy" in the novel). It was previously suggested, too, that Jim Casy predominantly prophesies whereas the Joads essentially act out such philosophy as we find in *The Grapes of Wrath*. But there is from the first an important line of communication open between Ma and Jim Casy; for Ma too is intuitive, and Ma is probably the most important symbol of love in the book. (To a lesser extent, Sairy Wilson also represents intuition, and human love.) It can be said in fact that Tom Joad's re-education and "conversion" to a new way of thinking is the result of his communication with both Jim Casy and Ma.

"Ma watched the preacher as he ate, and her eyes were questioning, probing and understanding. She watched him as though he were suddenly a spirit, not human any more, a voice out of the ground." Ma recognizes in Casy something different and detached, the quality which turns him more and more into a commentator and comforter, which makes possible such insights as he offers, for example, at Grampa's death (Chapter 13): Casy tells them, "Grampa didn't die tonight. He died the minute you took 'im off the place. . . . He didn' suffer none. Not after fust thing this mornin'. He's jus' stayin' with the lan'. He couldn' leave it." Jim Casy denies in good conscience that he has a God, but he practices brotherly love; this is why Sairy Wilson (Chapter 18) turns to him on her deathbed for truly human fellowship, a closeness to fellow humans she had once upon a time experienced through music, through singing. Sairy answers Casy, "You got a God. Don't make no difference if you don' know what he looks like." And after Casy had bowed his head and "talked to himself" instead of actually praying, she says, "That's good. That's what I needed. Somebody close enough—to pray."

God, then, is love, to Jim Casy and in actuality, to such figures as Ma and Sairy, because their *actions* are based on this love principle—intuitively, of course, rather than consciously. Jim Casy cannot in honesty claim he is sure of God, but he is sure of men and how they respond to brotherly love. Thus Casy is a pragmatist (pragmatism, in fact—the "is" thinking mentioned in the Introduction as one of Steinbeck's credos, is the third philosophical strand to be traced through *The Grapes of Wrath*. "Is" instead of "why" or "what should be"—this is what Jim Casy has voiced in Chapter 6 with his conviction that the emigrants are going to need help on their journey, but a kind of spiritual help geared to actualities rather than to preconceived notions: "Hope of heaven when their lives ain't lived?" Casy asks in exasperation. "They got to live before they can afford to die."

Ma, too, is a pragmatist, who takes things as they happen, and then of course acts from the love principle. She assesses (at the same time typically minimizing) her role to Al, for example (Chapter 13), as they ride along together. He has asked her timidly if she is scared about their new life. "A little," she honestly replies. "Only it ain't like scared so much. I'm jus' a settin' here waitin'. When somepin happens that I got to do somepin—I'll do it." Thus she does what she has to, staggeringly, when Granma dies as they cross the desert, lying all night beside the dead woman until she is certain that the family is safely across. Ma's act moves Jim Casy to an awed comment: "All night long, an' she was alone. . . . John, there's a woman so great with love—she scares me." Ma walks within the magic circle of brotherly love. But her response to the untimely death of Granma is no more than could have been expected from our introduction to her and her position in the Joad family unit in Chapter 8: "Her hazel eyes seemed to have experienced all possible tragedy and to have mounted pain and suffering like steps into a high calm and a superhuman understanding. She seemed to know, to accept, to welcome her position, the citadel of the family, the strong place that could not be taken. And since old Tom and the children could not know hurt or fear unless she acknowledged hurt and fear, she had practiced denying them in herself. And since, when a joyful thing happened, they looked to see whether joy was on her, it was her habit to build up laughter out of inadequate materials." (Note the almost biblical tone of the prose which describes Ma. There is in fact an Old Testament resonance to a sizeable portion of the prose in the novel.) From Ma's answer to a wondering remark of Tom's in this same chapter, we understand very well that she can be expected to "do what she has to," to fight, as it becomes necessary. Tom says with some amusement, "Ma, you never was like this before!" Ma replies sharply. "I never had my house pushed over. I never had my fambly stuck out on the road. I never had to sell—ever'thing."

INTERCHAPTER 9, AMASSED BITTERNESS: We have referred above to the growing social awareness of Jim ,Casy, Tom Joad, Ma, the development in them of an understanding that little people can gain power and security by acting as a group toward their common welfare. It is interesting that this idea, and the impetus for it, is generalized (just as all the interchapters deal with universally applicable social background, with unidentifiable actors in masks who seem to present in tableau the fate of all Joads, all Wilsons, all Davises). Of starting over again, the faceless, unseen "Everyman" of the Okies declares, "But you can't start. Only a baby can start. You and me—why, we're all that's been. The anger of a moment, the thousand pictures, that's us. This land, this red land, is us; and the flood years and the dust years and the drought years are us. We can't start again. The bitterness we sold to the junk man—he got it all right, but we have it still. And when the owner men told us to go, that's us; and when the tractor hit the house, that's us until we're dead. To California or any place—every one a drum major leading a parade of hurts, marching with out bitterness. And some day—the armies of bitterness will all be going the same way. And they'll all walk together, and there'll be a dead terror from it." (The image here is strongly suggestive of some of the lines from "Battle Hymn of the Republic," which Steinbeck had at one time intended to have printed along with the novel. The first four lines provide an especially vivid link with the unmistakeably socialistic vision offered here of the downtrodden poor arising in anger: "Mine eyes have seen the glory of the coming of the Lord,/ He is trampling out the vintage where the grapes of wrath are stored;/ He hath loosed the fateful lightening of his terrible swift sword,/ His truth is marching on.")

CHAPTERS 10, 11 AND 12

Having sold their remaining possessions dirt cheap, the Joads suddenly feel a sense of urgency about departing; they butcher the shoat, pack up everything, and are off in the dawn, leaving the forlorn Muley Graves standing in their dooryard watching. The desolation of the deserted houses and land is depicted in Chapter 11, an interchapter, which also contains harsh comments on the loveless mechanism of the tractors and their drivers: "when a horse stops work and goes into the barn there is a life and a vitality left, there is a breathing and a warmth, and the feet shift on the straw, and the jaws champ on the hay, and the ears and the eyes are alive. There is a warmth of life in the barn, and the heat and smell of life. But when the motor of a tractor stops, it is as dead as the ore it came from." Chapter 12 describes that "main migrant road," Highway 66; it marks the transition between roughly the first and second portions of the novel, introducing the journey or "exodus" (as the first part has been, in the biblical analogy, the "oppression in Egypt"). Highway 66 is a world in itself, and a vast, various one, reaching across the Texas Panhandle into the mountains, bleaching desert, then more mountains into the fantastic luxuriance of California. Trekking on 66 is no joke for drivers anxiously listening to motors, wheels or watching heat and oil gauges. Strange contradictory rumors about the Promised Land float from its two-bit service stations and restaurants. Over this pavement 250,000 people are in flight.

COMMENT

THE FAMILY UNIT: In Chapter 10 we see the Joad family unit functioning intact for almost the last time. Ma jokes communicatively with Tom as she scrubs clothes, and kids the spluttering and unbuttoned Grampa about "they don't let people run aroun' with their clothes unbutton' in California." In two different passages there is conveyed the sense that the men of the family still maintain their dignity, are still "whole." For example, Ma, powerful as she indubitably is, adheres to the ritual of letting the men decide if Jim Casy is to accompany them. "Ma looked to Tom to speak, because he was a man, but Tom did not speak. She let him have the chance that was his right, and then she said, 'Why, we'd be proud to have you. 'Course I can't say right now; Pa says all the men'll talk tonight and figger when we gonna start. I guess maybe we better not say till all the men come.' " And, as the truck returns from its ignominious mission of disposing of the remaining possessions, we see that "Al sat bent over the wheel, proud and serious and efficient, and Pa and Uncle John, as befitted the heads of the clan, had the honor seats beside the driver." Later in the evening, "the family met at the most important place, near the truck. The house was dead, and the fields were dead; but this truck was the active thing, the living principle." The clan is regrouping around its "new hearth, the living center of the family." Again, in the question of Casy's traveling with them, the ritual is preserved as they all wait out of politeness—"his position was honorary and a matter of custom"— for Grampa to voice his opinion. Afterwards the squatting men and the standing women may enter the discussion. There is an echo of Steinbeck's pamphlet title, *"Their Blood Is Strong,"* in Ma's prideful answer to whether or not they can feed an extra mouth. "It ain't kin we? It's will we? As far as 'kin, 'we can't do nothin', not go to California or nothin'; but as far as 'will,' why, we'll do what we will. An' as far as 'will' —it's a long time our folks been here and east before, an' I never heerd tell of no Joads or no Hazletts, neither, ever refusin' food an' shelter or a lift on the road to anybody that asked." Her tone makes Pa ashamed, and the issue of Jim Casy is of course settled.

JIM CASY, A PROPHET GROWS IN STATURE: Two characters who relate and communicate with Jim Casy—Ma and Tom—make further observations in Chapter 10 about what kind of man he seems to be. Ma reiterates in another way her feeling that he is changed, more spirit than man. "Watch the look in his eye," she declares. "He looks baptized. Got that

look they call lookin' through. He sure looks baptized. An'
a-walkin' with his head down, a-starin' at nothin' on the
groun'. There *is* a man that's baptized." It is as if she were
describing one who fasts and meditates (and indeed, a bit
later, Jim himself brings up in a half-deprecating manner the
analogy to Christ in the Wilderness), and to say that he gives
tangible evidence of his "baptism" is her highest praise. Jim
of course has discovered his "someplace to go." He has to go
where "the folks is goin'." Insisting that he will never "preach"
again, he tries to articulate his new-found "humanism." "I
ain't gonna try to teach 'em nothin'. I'm gonna try to learn.
Gonna learn why the folks walks in the grass, gonna hear 'em
talk, gonna hear 'em sing. . . . Gonna lay in the grass, open
an' honest with anybody that'll have me. Gonna cuss an' swear
an' hear the poetry of folks talkin'. All that's holy, all that's
what I didn' understand'." (Once more Jim's exuberant decla-
ration of love for the people is in the spirit of Walt Whitman.)
Tom Joad's contribution to the discussion of what is, or isn't
"preachin'" is ironically complimentary to Casy too:
"Preachin's a kinda tone a voice. . . . Preachin's bein' good to
folks when they wanna kill yar for it. Las' Christmas in Mc-
Alester, Salvation Army come an' done us good. Three solid
hours a cornet music, an' we set there. They was bein' nice to
us. But if one of us tried to walk out, we'd a-drawed solitary.
That's preachin'. . . . No, you ain't no preacher."

STEINBECK'S AGRARIAN THEORIES: One of the harshest
contrasts drawn so far by the author has been that of life close
to the land as opposed to cold mechanisms like tractors, their
inhuman drivers goggled and muzzled, and in the background
the indifferent manipulations of depersonalized ownership. In
this respect Chapter 11 can be cross-referenced to Chapter 5,
both interchapters. Here again the "deadness" of steel is contrasted to the warmth of land and animals and growing things.
The author is quite insistent on his point that man is not a
machine. "But the machine man, driving a dead tractor on
land he does not know and love, understands only chemistry;
and he is contemptuous of the land and of himself. When the
corrugated iron doors are shut, he goes home, and his home

is not the land." This has been said in greater length in Chapter 5 in describing the gloved and goggled man in the iron seat who has come to violate the land and its people. This man cannot touch, smell, feel. "He sat in an iron seat and stepped on iron pedals. He could not cheer or beat or curse or encourage the extension of his power, and because of this he could not cheer or whip or curse or encourage himself. He did not know or own or trust or beseech the land. . . . The land bore under iron, and under iron gradually died; for it was not loved or hated, it had no prayers or curses." Now, while this may be an exaggerated version of what happened ultimately to the land of the dust bowl, for it had simply been too long overworked in crops whether by hand or by machine, it is a powerful statement of what has been referred to as Steinbeck's agrarianism (or more specifically, Jeffersonian agrarianism). It is a form of democracy, and its focus is on the man's identification with the land. But actual contact with the land is essential for such a democracy to work, for it is in this closeness to the very cycles of growth, whether frustrating or gratifying, that a man's measure of himself, his dignity, resides. Thus a form of human erosion—and a disastrous one psychically—is being uprooted from the land as the dust bowl people were. As will be seen in comments following on later chapters, this philosophy—of the psychic hold the land gets on a man, of the meaningfulness of agrarianism as a way of life— is strongly urged throughout the novel.

CHAPTERS 13, 14 AND 15

"I dunno what we're comin' to," the fat filling station attendant on Highway 66 keeps saying, who has had people begging gasoline from him or trading chickens and bedsteads for it. And it turns out that he too is ready to pull out and go west. The first camp site for the Joads is a significant one, for they meet the Wilsons, with whom they form an alliance. Grampa dies abruptly of a stroke in their tent, and it is a blank page from their family Bible which is offered to record the facts that accompany Grampa to his grave in a glass jar, so that nobody will think he was murdered. The Wilsons' kindness is returned by Al's offer to help them repair their ailing car. A relationship has in fact been established by their acting together in sorrow, and they decide to travel together, which will enable them to space the load more easily over the two automobiles. Two ideas are significantly stressed in the short following interchapter: "The Western States are nervous under the beginning change," and "this is the beginning—from 'I' to 'We'." In other words, social revolution is in the air, clattering down Highway 66, where Mae and Al, along with innumerable others, run a restaurant whose reputation and economic security rests—quite legitimately—on what the truck drivers think of it. There is a poignant scene in which a migrant stops to buy ten cents worth of bread. Mae, tough as she tries to appear, ends by giving his children "nickel apiece" candy for a penny. Then the truck driver customers who observe her kindness tip her liberally on their way out.

COMMENT

FROM "I" TO "WE":   The steady emergence of a concept of "we"—group action in the public sense, human compassion for one's fellows in the personal sense—is really the whole thematic concentration of these three chapters. Steinbeck is developing more and more what he has taken pains to establish in the previous chapters: the anger and terror, accumulated bitterness, of these people—"the people in flight from the terror behind—strange things happen to them, some bitterly cruel and some so beautiful that the faith is refired forever"; the "beautiful happenings" that sometimes refire faith—the kindness of a toughened roadside waitress to a couple of yearning kids, repaid in turn by the tough truck drivers who observed the incident; a trailer built of junk and loaded with a family of twelve and their possessions, waiting in innocence and desperation on Highway 66 for a car to pull them to California, and a car does pick them up; a man like Jim Casy who feels the change in the air, senses that the people are "goin' someplace" and that they will need help. In short, given such a psychically charged situation, something will give, something has to give—and the direction will be one of love or hate. The first step toward "we" (not including the Joad family's joint decision to let Jim Casy accompany them) is the alliance with the Wilsons, founded on the deepest sort of kinship which is not of one's own blood: their acting together in a time of trouble (here, death; but it could have been birth too). Sairy Wilson voices her folk philosophy on the subject: "We're proud to help. I ain't felt so—safe in a long time. People needs—to help." This attitude is reinforced—formalized, we might say—by Jim Casy in his words for Grampa; in fact Jim's words seem to summarize his growing philosophy of humanism: "This here ol' man jus' lived a life an' jus' died out of it. I don't know whether he was good or bad, but that don't matter much. He was alive, an' that's what matters. An' now he's dead, an' that don't matter. Heard a fella tell a poem one time, an' he says 'All that lives is holy.' Got to thinkin', an' purty soon it means more than the words says. An' I wouldn' pray for a ol' fella that's dead. He's awright. He got a job to do, but it's all laid out for 'im an' there's on'y one way to do it. But us, we got a job to do, an' they's a thousan' ways, an' we don' know which one to take. An' if I was to pray, it'd be for the folks that don' know which way to turn." Again, Jim sounds like a pragmatist: the main thing is to be alive, and just as important, to help one's brother know "where to turn." Perhaps fittingly, it is Ma who solidifies the compact between the Joads and the Wilsons: "You won't be no burden. Each'll help each, an' we'll all git to California."

Thus interchapter 14 elaborates in a general way—partly through a kind of choric repetition (like a Greek chorus, which often fills in background, comments on the direction things are going, etc.). It is another way of saying the owners, the seemingly big and powerful, on one side and the little people on the other, when the two ideas are repeated: "the western land, nervous under the beginning change"; and "this is the beginning—from 'I' to 'we.'" The rest is elaboration: "The Western States, nervous as horses before a thunder storm. The great owners, nervous, sensing a change, knowing nothing of the nature of the change. The great owners, striking at the immediate thing, the widening government, the growing labor unity; striking at new taxes, at plans; not knowing these things are results, not causes." And the causes, the causes for the new "we" formations, put simply, are "a hunger in a stomach, multiplied a million times; a hunger in a single soul, hunger for joy and some security, multiplied a million times. . . ."

CHAPTERS 16, 17 AND 18

As the Joads and the Wilsons crawl on toward California in their two vehicles, there are more and more crises. The touring car of the Wilsons' breaks down, needing a new con-rod bearing, which will amount to a time-consuming repair job by Tom or Al. The Wilsons insist that the Joads go on without them. Tom offers an alternate plan, that the truck go ahead to California while they remain behind, Tom and Jim Casy, to repair the car and catch up with them. It is an appealing plan in that it would enable most of the adults to get work sooner. But, in her first and surprising show of violence, Ma puts her foot down. She amazes everybody with her "I ain't a'gonna go," and grabs a jack handle to back up her statement to Pa. Ma's strong instinct to survive requires that the family unit stay intact, a choice which takes precedence over mere expediency. Tom and Jim Casy stay behind to repair the car, which proves easier than they had anticipated, then join the family up the road at a camp, where there is more unpleasantness: a fifty cent charge, stubbornly applied to each car; a ragged man who is on his way back from California, having failed to make a living there.

The many roadside camps are described, where "in the evening a strange thing happened: the twenty families became one family, the children were the children of all. The loss of home became one loss. . . ." In the camps unwritten laws—"right"— emerge, through practical experience and common sense. Passed by the border patrol, they enter California with a prospect of the Painted Desert, to be crossed. They encamp by a river to rest for a night crossing, and there are more setbacks and crises: another man on his way back from California, saying it's nice country but it "was stole a long time ago"; a fanatical Jehovite woman, like a bad omen, who frightens Rosasharn and strains Ma's nerves, tight from tending the ailing Granma—Ma is forced to assert, "We ain't gonna have no meetin' in this here tent." Ma's second moment of violent anger comes in her confrontation of the policeman in khaki and boots and pistol who stops at the tent and informs her they must get out; this time she grabs an iron skillet to reinforce her scornful words to the challenger. The men bathe in the river, where the strange and silent Noah informs Tom he will remain by the river and catch fish, instead of going on with them. When it is time to start into the desert, it is discovered that Sairy Wilson, never well, is at last too ill to go on. Jim Casy comforts her, and most reluctantly they leave the Wilsons behind. At midnight they reach an inspection station in the desert, where there is a demand to look over their possessions, to unload the vehicles. Again Ma steps forth with a kind of hysterically dogged refusal to allow the search, insisting that Granma is too sick; yet when Tom speeds up to the next town, Barstow, where the inspectors have said a doctor can be found, Ma begs them to go on across. In the dawn they come out of the desert, creep into the mountains and at last pause to get out and look down into the green valleys of California. It is then that they discover that Granma has lain dead in Ma's arms all through the night.

COMMENT

TOM JOAD, ORIENTATION TOWARD CONVERSION: In his response to Jim Casy's social prophecy, as they work together on the old sedan, Tom Joad is common sensical—a pragmatist too, we might say—and somewhat individualist— to each his own. Just as Tom refuses to look ahead, and worry, Jim Casy is insisting that things are moving ahead anyhow. "If ya listen," he says, "you'll hear a movin', an' a sneakin', an' a rustlin', an'—an' a res'lessness. They's stuff goin' on that the folks doin' it don't know nothin' about—yet. They's gonna come somepin outa all these folks goin' wes'— outa all their farms lef' lonely. They's gonna come a thing that's gonna change the whole country." This is when Tom repeats "I'm still layin' my dogs down one at a time," and "I climb fences when I got fences to climb." Yet Tom is being pulled more and more into the changes, and into meditating about the changes, toward that end point when, Jim Casy having in effect laid down his life for Tom, Tom becomes a disciple and a fighter. Furthermore, Tom's strain of stoic realism is useful to his growing philosophical awareness; for example the manner in which he shakes up the whining, self-pitiful one-eyed service station attendant by trying to show him how he really appears and how he could appear seems to have some effect, for he asks Tom softly, "Think—somebody'd like—me?" And at the end of Chapter 18, Tom speaks to his parents stoically but compassionately about Grampa and Granma, now dead. His mother looks at the green and gold country of California lying before them and observes how "purty" it is, wishing the old folks could have seen it. Tom's answer parallels Jim Casy's earlier observation about how Grampa really died, in his heart, before ever leaving the homestead. "They was too old. They wouldn't of saw nothin' that's here. Grampa would a been a-seein' the Injuns an' the prairie country when he was a young fella. An' Granma would a remembered an' seen the first home she lived in. They was too ol'. Who's really seein' it is Ruthie an' Winfiel'."

DETERIORATING UNITY, MA FIGHTS DESTRUCTIVE ELEMENTS: We have seen that Ma's anger and violence are aroused when there is a real crisis involving preserving and protecting her family: she rises up against Pa with a jack handle to prevent him from separating the two loaded cars as they travel; she orders out of her tent the fanatical Jehovite woman because she threatens to become a disruptive influence, especially to Rosasharn, since her ideas of sin are a bit rigid and upsetting to the pregnant girl; she grabs an iron skillet and is about to take a swing of indignation at the cold and contemptuous uniformed stranger who intrudes upon the privacy of the tent and calls her a strangely derogatory name, "Okie"; and she takes her solitary initiative in the middle of the desert at night to prevent the inspectors from unloading the truck and discovering Granma's death before they are safely across the desert.

Ma's violence can be looked upon as a last-ditch stand, as she senses the growing desperateness and futility of the situation.

Her awareness that the family seems to be falling apart and her hidden feelings of helplessness at the frustrations brought from outside forces are seen in these chapters too. Ma never gives way—publicly. But after the iron skillet incident, "Rose of Sharon watched her secretly. And when she saw Ma fighting with her face, Rose of Sharon closed her eyes and pretended to be asleep." Ma is dazed at Tom's news of Noah's disappearance, turning "stunned eyes toward the river. 'I jus' can't seem to think no more,' " is her answer. As they all prepared to leave that night, because the policeman has stated that they must be out of there by morning, Ma voices to Tom—or to nobody in particular—her sense of lowered morale. " 'I pray God we gonna get some res'. I pray Jesus we gonna lay down in a nice place.' The sun sank toward the baked and broken hills to the west. The pot over the fire bubbled furiously. Ma went under the tarpaulin and came out with an apronful of potatoes, and she dropped them into the boiling water. 'I pray God we gonna be let to wash some clothes. We ain't never been dirty like this. Don't even wash potatoes 'fore we boil 'em. I wonder why? Seems like the heart's took out of us.' " And, since Ma is the core or center of the family, her reflections ring grimly true.

PRAGMATISM: The pragmatic attitudes seen in Tom Joad and Jim Casy are reflected in the first experiences of the families at the campsites. That is, as the families adjust to the new and very different life of the road and the camp, fashioning unwritten laws or rights to fit the present circumstances, they are behaving pragmatically. "The families learned what rights must be observed—the right of privacy in the tent; the right to keep the black past hidden in the heart; the right to talk and to listen; the right to refuse help or to accept, to offer help or to decline it. . . ." These are positive rights, just as there are also prohibitions, negative rights, which come to be understood: do not intrude upon a man's privacy; keep quiet while the camp sleeps; the customary protection against theft and murder must prevail. It is important to emphasize again from time to time this philosophical strand of the novel—pragmatism—in order to realize that those people who could learn a new way, who proved most flexible, had the best chance of survival. And in such an attitude the people might even have a weapon against "the owners," those awaiting so "nervously" in the West, those who in effect are mentally "running scared." As the discouraged fellow who is on his way back east points out, "They hate you 'cause they're scairt. They know a hungry fella gonna get food even if he got to take it. They know that fallow lan's a sin an' somebody' gonna take it." These men, the owners, are not flexible, are not pragmatists, as was suggested in Chapter 14; for they strike out in panic at the "immediate thing," not able to see the causes for the sullenly rebellious army of people creeping across the West. Steinbeck seems to be saying that ownership "freezes" these people into *in*flexibility; thus they fear the two men squatting in a ditch, conferring, "figgering," because it bodes change and revolution —they must separate these two men, and fear them, without comprehension. The comment in this chapter applies throughout: "If you who own the things people must have could understand this, you might preserve yourself. . . . But that you cannot know. For the quality of owning freezes you forever into 'I,' and cuts you off forever from the 'we.' "

CHAPTERS 19, 20, 21 AND 22

As a transition into the third part of the novel, the sojourn in California, there is the historical/social information provided in Chapter 19—the land of California stolen from the Mexicans who were weaker, the first squatters who thus became owners, and later, exploiters of other weak people: Chinese, Japanese, Mexicans, Filipinos—and Okies. The Joads are still hurt over Granma's "county" burial—they could spare but $5 for her painted box—as they set up camp in their first Hooverville and learn immediately that work is scarce and constant harassment from the local police is to be expected. Connie Rivers experiences at this point his definitive disillusionment, declaring sullenly, "If I'd of knowed it would be like this I wouldn' of came. I'd a studied nights 'bout tractors back home an' got me a three-dollar job." He disappears into the woods not to return. Ma is horrified by the cluster of hungry children who gather around her stew pot, in which there is barely enough to feed her own family; her dilemma between compassion and practicability is touching. A man named Floyd, whom Al helps with grinding the points on his car, fills him and Tom in on the situation. There is trouble, when a contractor, accompanied by a deputy sheriff, comes into the camp ostensibly looking for workers; the way the authorities operate by intimidation and coercion is demonstrated when Floyd questions their legal authority, asking for assurance about wages (since they invariably go down when the number of applicants increases, a situation the owners purposely set up), and is called "red" and "agitator"—by witness of the deputy—and arrested. He hits the deputy, runs, is shot at (a woman's hand catches the .45 bullet); Tom and Jim Casy enter the fray, and in the end Jim Casy takes the blame, and the arrest, for Tom, who had hit the deputy from behind. It is one of the occasions when Uncle John is so troubled, supposedly by his shame at not acting as Jim Casy did, that he has to get drunk on some of his little store of money. Aware that the camp is to be burned out before morning—a common occurrence—the Joads head for the incredibly decent government camp at Weedpatch. For the almost idyllic period of their stay in this government camp—which is run along the lines of the modern Israeli *kibbutz*—the family pride of the Joads is restored. From the moment Tom drives the truck through the entrance, barely avoiding damage to the old car because of a hump placed purposely in the roadway to cause drivers to slow down for the children often playing there, the atmosphere is different, decent and human. There are Sanitary Units with hot water and toilet facilities (the experiments of young Ruthie and Winfield with the curiosity of a flushing toilet—when it flushes, they assume it is broken—are pathetically amusing), a series of elected committees which govern the camp community, and a regular social life—square dances on Saturday, known to the people around (for the camp people may invite friends among the small farmers) as the only dance to which a man can bring his wife and children. They can work out, if they wish, the dollar a week the camp costs, and they can get credit through a co-op plan for up to $5 at the camp grocery, where the prices are also fair (instead of invariably higher than "in town," as at all other camps). Since the camp officially is "United States" rather than "California," no police are permitted to enter unless there is a riot. Ma eagerly sets about pulling her family back together, getting them clean and well-fed, and anticipating with a nervous womanly pride the visit of the Ladies Committee. Perhaps she sums up the government camp—what it means to be addressed as "Mrs. Joad" again, as well as what the author is saying in terms of social theory—by her sigh, "Why, I feel like people again."

COMMENT

AGRARIANISM OVER CAPITALISM: Chapter 19 fills in historical information of social significance about the settling of California, explaining how the land taken from the Mexicans, once planted and harvested and inhabited, became "possession, and possession was ownership." But the real purpose of this interchapter is to trace the insidious process by which love of the land was replaced by "shopkeeping" and "manufacturing" attitudes toward the land. (And it is well to recall here that the author by his long residence in California from childhood was in a position to comment on these changes.) "And all their love was thinned with money, and all their fierceness dribbled away in interest until they were no longer farmers at all, but little shopkeepers of crops, little manufacturers who must sell before they can make. Then those farmers who were not good shopkeepers lost their land to good shopkeepers. No matter how clever, how loving a man might be with earth and growing things, he could not survive if he were not also a good shopkeeper. And as time went on, the business men had the farms, and the farms grew larger, but there were fewer of them." As farming became an industry, the crops changed more and more to concentration on money-making types, and there was increasing exploitation of workers used to low wages —foreigners, outsiders, although the Okies fiercely felt they were Americans, in America seven generations back, having fought in the Revolution and the Civil War. The sympathetic reassertion here of the agrarian way of life is evidenced by the crimes enumerated: the "imported slaves"—"they live on rice and beans, the business men said. They don't need much. They wouldn't know what to do with good wages. Why, look how they live. Why, look what they eat. And if they get funny —deport them"; the crime of fallow land where people are hungry—"And a homeless hungry man, driving the roads with his wife beside him and his thin children in the back seat, could look at the fallow fields which might produce food but not profit, and that man could know how a fallow field is a sin and the unused land a crime against the thin children"; and, "oranges to be dumped if the price was low"—a situation devastatingly elaborated in Chapter 25, which begins "the spring is beautiful in California" but ends with the bitter-as-gall statement of facts: "Burn coffee for fuel in the ships. Burn corn to keep warm, it makes a hot fire. Dump potatoes in the rivers and place guards along the banks to keep the hungry people from fishing them out. Slaughter the pigs and bury them, and let the putrescence drip down into the earth."

OAKIES: Steinbeck expands a little in Chapter 19 on the "concept" of "Okies"—the reasons of their "Americanness" (as contrasted to the Chinese, Japanese, Filipinos and Mexican migrants) as well as of their desperation which might contrive to amass them into a social force. One paragraph in particular assesses their accumulating grievances, an accumulation which we observe grows more and more explosive in the third section of the book, culminating in the various disasters and decisions at the end. "They were hungry, and they were fierce. And they had hoped to find a home, and they found only hatred. Okies—the owners hated them because the owners knew they were soft and the Okies strong, that they were fed and the Okies hungry; and perhaps the owners had heard from their grandfathers how easy it is to steal land from a soft man if you are fierce and hungry and armed. . . . And in the towns, the storekeepers hated them because they had no money to spend. There is no shorter path to a storekeeper's contempt. . . . The town men, little bankers, hated Okies because there was nothing to gain from them." It is a way of saying, "their blood is strong," and they may turn out to be the very ones who will rise effectively in social protest.

THE SOCIAL LESSON, AMELIORATION OR EXPLOSION:
One anecdote, well depicted, serves as well as any to measure the increasing frustrations of downtrodden people like the Okies: the patch of garden in the Jimson weeds—"Now and then a man tried; crept on the land and cleared a piece, trying like a thief to steal a little richness from the earth. Secret gardens hidden in the weeds. A package of carrot seeds and a few turnips. Planted potato skins, crept out in the evening secretly to hoe in the stolen earth." (Notice the poetic quality through sound effects, consonance and assonance.) But the deputy sheriff kicks off the carrot tops and tramples the turnip greens and remarks, "Did ya see his face when we kicked them turnips out? Why, he'd kill a fella soon's he look at him. We got to keep these here people down or they'll take the country." Fear piled on top of fear, anger on top of anger. Or the representative newsclipping: "In Lawrenceville a deputy sheriff evicted a squatter, and the squatter resisted, making it neces-

sary for the officer to use force. The eleven-year-old son of the squatter shot and killed the deputy with a .22 rifle."

As they camp in their first California Hooverville, Tom Joad, who has heard from Floyd Knowles the harsh facts of their situation, comes to talk to Jim Casy about it. As usual Jim Casy has had it "figgered" out for a long time. "Listen all the time. That's why I been thinkin'. Listen to people a-talkin', an' purty soon I hear the way folks are feelin'. Goin' on all the time. I hear 'em an' feel 'em; an' they're beating their wings like a bird in an attic. Gonna bust their wings on a dusty winda tryin' ta get out." (Jim reiterates, incidentally, on this occasion his latter-day conviction of the inadequacy of religion and prayer for such real-life problems: "I use ta think that'd cut 'er. . . . Use ta rip off a prayer an' all the troubles'd stick to that prayer like flies on flypaper, an' the prayer'd go a-sailin' off, a-takin' them troubles along. But it don' work no more.")

Tom, in his reflections voiced to the somewhat demoralized and skeptical Floyd Knowles, puts his finger once again on the concept of group action. "Well, s'pose them people got together an' says, 'Let 'em rot.' Wouldn' be long 'fore the price went up, by God!" As Floyd points out, such actions have been tried, and stopped by the greater power of the local officials. But lurking in this conversation and others, of course, is the idea of unions and striking, which Jim Casy comes to believe in enough to fight for and lose his life for.

The ideal for these people is presented in Weedpatch, the humane government camp, where the Joads begin to feel like people again and hope is temporarily restored. Washed, clean, fed, warm, almost comfortable for a change, Ma, the spokesman for endurance—"Why, Tom, we're the people that live. They ain't gonna wipe us out. Why, we're the people—we go on"—begins to hope and plan again, as if such feelings are natural to humans when they have a modest sense of well-being: "Wouldn' it be nice if the menfolks all got work? Them a-workin', an' a little money comin' in? Them a-workin', an'

us a-workin' here, an' all them nice people. Fust thing we get
a little ahead I'd get me a little stove—nice one. They don'
cost much. . . . An' Sat'dy night we'll go to the dancin'. They
says you can invite folks if you want. I wisht we had some
frien's to invite." For at Weedpatch people pay if they can,
and work it out if they can't. And those who can't go out into
the fields are assigned other jobs, such as caring for small
children. The government is formed out of the people themselves. A brilliant example of the psychological efficacy of
such a social structure, as the author sees it, is provided in the
incident of Ruthie's rude intrusion on the game of croquet
going on among the children. In profound childish mistrust of
her own social acceptability, exhibiting the hostility which is
the inevitable outcome of the rejection and diminished self-
esteem increasingly thrust upon her family and therefore upon
her, she insists upon playing in the game presently in progress,
in spite of the assurance from the pig-tailed little girl that she
can play "next game." She slaps the girl and wrests the mallet
from her. At this point the elderly lady observing all intervenes
and tells the children to let Ruthie play, by which she means
that they *all* drop their mallets and exit from the court, leaving
Ruthie to play alone, in false and lonely satisfaction. At length
she flings down the mallet and flies home in tears. The old
woman says wisely to the children returning to the court (one
could only wish most play supervisors were as wise as she,
and question, critically, whether Steinbeck is idealizing a bit):
"When she comes back an' wants to be decent, you let her.
You was mean yourself, Amy." But the basic point is valid:
people, lives, however damaged, can be rehabilitated, through
attitudes which are at once pragmatic and compassionate.

Also, in the description of the Weedpatch system of government, the distinction between "charity" and "communal living"
is carefully established. The amusing core of the story is that
somebody has been stealing toilet paper from Unit Four. "We
got our troubles with toilet paper," says Jessie Bullitt, member
of the Ladies' Committee of Sanitary Unit Number Four.
"Rule says you can't take none away from here. . . . Whole
camp chips in for toilet paper. . . . Number Four is usin' more

than any other. Somebody's a-stealin' it. Come up in general ladies' meetin'. Ladies' side, Unit Number Four is usin' too much. Come right up in meetin'!" But this time three little girls are not cutting paper dolls from it, as on the last occasion; for a "flushed, perspiring woman" steps to a doorway to "confess" that her five children have probably been using too much because they have all had the skitters (diarrhea), from eating green grapes, because they are short of money. At which the admirable Jessie Bullitt announces, "Now you hol' up your head. That ain't no crime. You jes waltz right over t' the Weed-patch store an' git you some groceries. The camp got twenty dollars' credit there. You git yourself fi' dollars' worth. An' you kin pay it back to the Central Committee when you git work." To Mrs. Joyce's protest that "we ain't never took no charity," there is the vigorous reply that such is not charity, for the credit belongs to the camp jointly and may be dispensed to anyone. This in contrast to Annie Littlefield's embittered comments on the Salvation Army, where her family was made to feel it *was* charity: "Las' winter; an' we was a-starvin'—me an' the little fellas. An' it was a-rainin'. Fella tol' us to go to the Salvation Army. . . . We was hungry—they made us crawl for our dinner. They took our dignity. . . . Mis' Joad, we don't allow nobody in this camp to build theirself up that-a-way. We don't allow nobody to give nothing to another person. They can give it to the camp, an' the camp can pass it out. We won't have no charity!" Her voice was fierce and hoarse. "I hate 'em," she said. "I ain't never seen my man beat before, but them—them Salvation Army done it to 'im." (It is probably the *concept* of charity with its damage to the psyche which is being lambasted here more than the Salvation Army per se.)

PROSE STYLE IN CHAPTER 19: It was suggested earlier that Steinbeck's style is here and there indebted to the Old Testament. One of Steinbeck's critics, for example—Peter Lisca—has arranged in phrases, like poetry, some of the lines in Chapter 11, which sets forth the author's agrarian philosophy; the effect is that of reading from a page of the Old Testament. It is interesting that in Chapter 19, which also deals with agrarianism, the love of the land contrasted to merely "shop-keeping" the land and working it only with an eye toward larger and larger profit, the lines read similarly and could be arranged thus:

And all the time the farms grew larger and the owners fewer.
And there were pitifully few farmers on the land anymore.
And the imported serfs were beaten and frightened
And starved until some went home again,
And some grew fierce and were killed or driven from the country.
And the farms grew larger and the owners fewer.
And the crops changed.
Fruit trees took the place of grain fields,
And vegetables to feed the world spread out on the bottoms:
Lettuce, cauliflower, artichokes, potatoes—stoop crops.
A man may stand to use a scythe, a plow, a pitchfork;
But he must crawl like a bug between the rows of lettuce,
He must bend his back and pull his long bag between the cotton rows,
He must go on his knees like a penitent across a cauliflower patch.
And it came about that. . . .

Steinbeck is clearly influenced by Biblical style, and the analogy between the Joads and Israel in Egypt: as we have seen, the three parts of the novel divide roughly into oppression, exodus and the land of Canaan.

CHAPTERS 23, 24 AND 25

Chapter 23, gently ironic, placed between those chapters which describe the Weedpatch idyl, depicts the pleasures of the migrant people. "The migrant people, scuttling for work, scrabbling to live, looked always for pleasure, dug for pleasure, manufactured pleasure, and they were hungry for amusement. Sometimes amusement lay in speech, and they climbed up their lives with jokes." Or there were the folk three: harmonica, fiddle and guitar. And if a man had a little money, there was liquor, "the hard edges gone, and the warmth. Then there was no loneliness, for a man could people his brain with friends, and he could find his enemies and destroy them. . . . Failures dulled and the future was no threat. And hunger did not skulk about. . . ." Chapter 24 is another cheerful interlude in the lives of the Joads, except for the incident at the dance of the three young men who have been hired to start a fight and cause trouble for the government camp. Saturday is wash day: first the children, then the men, last the women, get clean and ready for the night's dancing. There is a poignant moment when Rose of Sharon—young, married, pregnant and deserted —expresses to Ma her fearful longing to attend the dance. Ma as usual fixes things; that is, she arranges it so that the lonely girl can stay out of trouble. "Know what you an' me's gonna do? We're a-goin' to that dance, an' we're a-gonna set there and watch. If anybody says to come dance—why, I'll say you ain't strong enough. I'll say you're poorly. An' you can hear the music an' all like that." The men meanwhile plot to thwart the anticipated attempt from the outside to disrupt their camp, and they worry together about job prospects. Chapter 25 speaks for itself its contrasts: the language of growth, which is beautiful—"the spring is beautiful in California"—at war with the language of destruction, which is ugly—"burn coffee. . . . dump potatoes. . . . slaughter pigs."

COMMENT

SOCIAL PROTEST THROUGH GROUP ACTION: The successful routing of the three potential rioters at the Saturday dance in Weedpatch government camp is of course an instance of the effectiveness of group action, made possible, we ought to note in passing, by the sense of fellowship demonstrated by the small farmer Mr. Thomas who leaks the plan to Tom and his colleagues who work for him briefly (Thomas of course is one of those being squeezed out by price-setting and other power moves of the bigger operators). And, although their frustrations remain just as great as ever, once the resolve is made to handle the incident and the three intruders without violence, that resolve is upheld. Afterwards, though, the men squat together discussing the "change a-comin' " which all of them are just about agreed upon by now. For Pa, so far pretty passive, says "They's change a-comin'. I don' know what. Maybe we won't live to see her. But she's a-comin'. They's a res'less feelin'." And the man in the black hat relates the impressive anecdote of the revolt of the mountain people against the rubber companies in Akron, Ohio. The chronicle of persecution of the "outsiders" by the local people seems to have been the same: a union formed, the great hue and cry of Red!; storekeepers and legioners and preachers out in military drill with pick handles. Then, "Well, sir—it was las' March, an' one Sunday five thousan' of them mountain men had a turkey shoot outside of town. Five thousan' of 'em jes' marched through town with their rifles. An' they had their turkey shoot, an' then they marched back. An' that's all they done. Well, sir, they ain't been no trouble sence then. These here citizens committees give back the pick handles, an' the storekeepers keep their stores, an' nobody been clubbed nor tarred an' feathered, an' nobody been killed." In the silence that follows, Black Hat brings forth his inevitable point: "They're gettin' purty mean out here. Burned that camp an' beat up folks. I been thinkin'. All our folks got guns. I been thinkin' maybe we ought to git up a turkey shootin' club an' have meetin's ever' Sunday." A lot of such "thinkin'," and the moving restless feet of the men who listen, and we are not far from the actions which will be initiated by men like Jim Casy who at length take it upon themselves to act out what they have thought out.

It is fitting that the author includes his most vigorous and poetic social protest statement in the following chapter (25). The ironic contrast is apparent. The quite paradisical vision of spring in California, the ripening of all growing things for the good harvest—"the first tendrils of the grapes, swelling from the old gnarled vines, cascade down to cover the trunks"; "petals drop from the fruit trees and carpet the earth with pink and white"; "the centers of the blossoms swell and grow and color." The earnest men "of understanding and knowledge and skill" who experiment and watch and nurture toward the perfect crop. Then the awesome awareness that such quickening and ripening has been born and nourished to rot: cherries, prunes, pears, grapes. The price is too low to pay wages to pick them; the wine must be cheaply and cheatingly made, with rotten or wasp-stung grapes and chemicals. The little farmers will be inevitably overcome by debt. Decay, physical and moral, is the keynote of the atmosphere. The chapter concludes on such crimes against nature and men most bitterly and eloquently. "There is a crime here that goes beyond denunciation. There is a sorrow here that weeping cannot symbolize. There is a failure here that topples all our success. The fertile earth, the straight tree rows, the sturdy trunks, and the ripe fruit. And children dying of pellagra must die because a profit cannot be taken from an orange. . . . The people come with nets to fish for potatoes in the river, and the guards hold them back; they come in rattling cars to get the dumped oranges, but the kerosene is sprayed. And they stand still and watch the potatoes float by, listen to the screaming pigs being killed in a ditch and covered with quicklime, watch the mountains of oranges slop down to a putrefying ooze; and in the eyes of the people there is the failure; and in the eyes of the hungry there is a growing wrath. In the souls of the people the grapes of wrath are filling and growing heavy, growing heavy for the vintage."

CHAPTERS 26, 27 AND 28

Life at the Weedpatch camp could breed apathy, however, out of its very decency: although there was no work to be found in the area, the families could not bear to leave. But one night after supper Ma pins down her men to discussing specifically just what they are going to do now. She reminds them of what they have avoided bringing out in the open: Winfield jerking and twisting in his sleep; "one day' more grease an' two days' flour, an' ten potatoes"; meals of fried dough. But it is a psychological and emotional impasse: the men claim, in truth, that "we been a-lookin', Ma. Been walkin' out sence we can't use the gas no more. Been goin' in ever' gate, walkin' up to ever' house. . . . Puts a weight on ya. Goin' out lookin' for somepin you know you ain't gonna find." Ma's position is just as clear, and true: "You ain't got the right to get discouraged. This here fambly's goin' under. You jus' ain't got the right." The upshot of the conference is that they are up and out of the camp before dawn the next morning. At the advice of a smiling well-dressed man in a roadster who directs them they head 40 miles north to the Hooper ranch to pick peaches. Although the tight security check of name and license by the armed deputies strikes them as strange when they enter the ranch premises and set up in a dirty little one-room shack, it is only later that they become aware that they are "strikebreakers," that they have been hired in the place of exasperated men who joined together in rebellion against the 2½¢ a box they were offered to pick peaches. But they know it is an unfriendly place, with inhabitants who seem ashamed of being there. When Ma takes the hard-earned slip for one dollar—the joint earnings of the family for the day—to the man at the little store, she discovers painfully that all items are overpriced in comparison to town shopping, and the dollar is easily eaten up in one night's dinner.

Tom walks out to explore the curious situation after supper and comes across a tent hidden in a deep ravine, from which to his surprise emerges Jim Casy. For Jim the time in jail has been like Christ's days in the wilderness, he says, for he has finally worked out things in his mind. He reasons that even decent people will steal when there is absolutely no other way to get what they need. And he relates how one day when sour beans were served the prisoners, their mass protest obtained results. Casy leaves his point up to Tom to figure out, but it turns out that the preacher has gained a small reputation for himself in the current strike and union activities. This is unfortunately proved by the violence which follows. The nervous men hear noises and when they go to look, come upon two searchers with pick handles. They are after Jim Casy, whom they recognize. One of them crushes Casy's skull with the pick handle, as he is saying, "Listen, you fellas don' know what you're doin'. You're helpin' to starve kids. . . . You don' know what you're a-doin'." As Tom looks at the preacher, who is undoubtedly dead, he knows what to do. He grabs the pick handle, pounds at the man who has assailed Jim Casy, and, struck a glancing blow, makes an escape down the stream. Tom creeps into the shack and lies in pain with his crushed nose until the dawn, when he is obliged to relate to Ma what has happened. The first day he hides there in the house (for it is certain then that he has killed the deputy); after that the family apprehensively moves on, stopping at a point where they hope to pick some cotton, and hiding Tom in a culvert with a blanket. They take up their last residence in some boxcars, sharing the long boxcar with the Wainwrights. While the cotton lasts they are able to earn well and eat well. However, because little Ruthie in an argument with another child over some Cracker Jacks has revealed that her brother is a killer hiding out, it is considered too dangerous for Tom to remain there, and Ma bids him a painful farewell. He tells her that, although he hopes to keep from getting killed, he intends to do now "what Casy done." As Ma walks back to the camp a man catches up with her and offers a small picking job to her and her family. It turns out to be the last picking they get. As they finish the job and start back to camp the next day, the rains begin. Yet life goes on: Al Joad and Aggie Wainwright are engaged, and Rose of Sharon's time is almost due.

COMMENT

TOM JOAD, THE NEW PROPHET AND LEADER: In Chapter 26 Ma explains that she has just been "a-treadin' " on Pa to make him mad, to get him to act, but that it is really Tom she leans on. "You got more sense, Tom. 'I don' need to make you mad. I got to lean on you. Them others—they're kinda strangers, all but you. You won't give up, Tom." Perhaps because he is a pragmatist—because he *has* "got more sense," Tom takes the job reluctantly, asserting "I don' like it. I wanta go out like Al. An' I wanta get mad like Pa, an' I wanta get drunk like Uncle John." But Ma insists that Tom is not like the others, never has been—he is "more than himself." "Ever'thing you do is more'n you. When they sent you up to prison I knowed it. You're spoke for." This is the same as to say, especially since Jim Casy has just died a martyr's death, that Tom is the new prophet. This is borne out in the parting scene between Ma and Tom, where he describes to her the death of Casy, and tells her what he is going to do. In his hiding place in the brush he has been thinking about all the things Casy ever said (it can be said, in fact, that when Tom goes forth from the solitary ravine he is emerging from his own Biblical "wilderness"). As Tom sets forth his thoughts to Ma it is clear that he has got hold of Jim Casy's concept of the "oversoul," and of Jim's late conviction of the promise of group action. "But now I been thinkin' what he said, an' I can remember—all of it. Says one time he went out in the wilderness to find his own soul, an' he foun' he didn' have no soul that was his'n. Says he foun' he jus' got a little piece of a great big soul. Says a wilderness ain't no good, 'cause his little piece of a soul wasn't no good 'less it was with the rest, an' was whole. Funny how I remember. Didn' think I was even listenin'. But I know now a fella ain't no good alone." That Tom remarks he wasn't listening, he thought, is another hint that his knowledge has been "intuitive," almost "divine revelation." (It should also be pointed out that Tom's "cave" is a womblike place, his state there is somewhat "pre-natal," and his emergence, especially after the confrontation with Ma, is like a rebirth.) He has absorbed Jim Casy's message that "two are better than one," and now relates it to the agrarian philosophy and the concept of group action. "I been thinkin' how it was in that gov'ment camp, how our folks took care a theirselves, an' if they was a fight they fixed it theirself; an' they wasn't no cops wagglin' their guns, but they was better order than them cops ever give. I been a-wonderin' why we can't do that all over. Throw out the cops that ain't our people. All work together for our own thing—all farm our own lan'." When Ma expresses her fears that he will kill or be killed, he reverts to the concept of the Oversoul. "Well, maybe like Casy says, a fella ain't got a soul of his own, but on'y a piece of a big one—an' then. . . . Then it don' matter. Then I'll be all aroun' in the dark. I'll be ever'where—wherever you look. Wherever they's a fight so hungry people can eat, I'll be there. Wherever they's a cop beatin' up a guy, I'll be there. If Casy knowed, why, I'll be in the way guys yell when they're mad an'—I'll be in the ways kids laugh when they're hungry an' they know supper's ready. An' when our folks eat the stuff they raise an' live in the houses they build—why, I'll be there." Tom's speech is pretty much Biblical paraphrase—he has practically said "Lo, I am with you always, even unto the ends of the earth"—and he has declared his spiritual oneness with his brothers, moving beyond personal material considerations to action from ethical principle and inner conviction. (Jim Casy's martyrdom, incidentally, and his stature as Christ-like prophet, has been made pretty clear through Tom's description of his death to Ma, who demands to know, so she can "figger how it was"—in other words, assure herself about Tom's innocence or guilt. Tom repeats Casy's last words: "You got no right to starve people. . . . You don' know what you're a-doin'." As if to make no mistake Ma too repeats the words: "Tha's what he said—'You don' know what you're doin' '?" So we have a paraphrase of Christ's last words on the cross, "Forgive them, Lord, for they know not what they do.")

CONTROL OF THE FAMILY: In the last chapters of the book

Ma has taken over control of the family, although she remains compassionate in the role. In Chapter 26, after she has forced the menfolk to consider what moves they must make to survive, Pa sniffles: "Seems like times is changed. Time was when a man said what we'd do. Seems like women is tellin' now. Seems like it's purty near time to get out a stick." Ma answers, "You get your stick, Pa. Times when they's food an' a place to set, then maybe you can use your stick an' keep your skin whole. But you ain't a-doin' your job, either a-thinkin' or a-workin'." At this point Ma contends afterward to Tom that she did it to "rile" Pa, that things are still all right. "He's all right. He ain't beat. He's like as not to take a smack at me." But later, when she begs Tom to stay with them, after he has killed the deputy, her reasons indicate her doubts: "Tom! They's a whole lot I don' un'erstan'. . . . They was a time when we was on the lan'. They was a boundary to us then. Ol' folks died off, an' little fellas come, an' we was always one thing—we was the fambly—kinda whole and clear. An' now we ain't clear no more. I can't get straight. They ain't nothin' keeps us clear. Al—he's a-hankerin' an' a-jibbitin' to go off on his own. An' Uncle John is jus' a-draggin' along. Pa's lost his place. He ain't the head no more. We're crackin' up, Tom. There ain't no fambly now." And at length, in Chapter 28, the issue is brought out into the open between Pa and Ma. When the Wainwrights express their fears to the Joads about the deepening relationship between Aggie and Al, Ma answers, "Pa'll talk to Al. Or if Pa won't, I will." Later she apologizes to Pa. "I didn' mean no harm a-sayin' I'd talk to Al." "I know," is Pa's quiet answer. "I ain't no good any more. Spen' all my time a-thinkin' how it use' ta be." He goes on to reflect how, even though as Ma points out, the new land is "purtier," he has been escaping dreamily into the past. Of this new but painful land he remarks, "I never even see it, thinkin' how the willow's los' its leaves now. Sometimes figgerin' to mend that hole in the south fence. Funny! Woman takin' over the fambly. Woman sayin' we'll do this here, an' we'll go there. An' I don' even care." These are desolate words, to which Ma answers with intuition and compassion. "Woman can change better'n a man. Woman got all her life in

her arms. Man got it all in his head. Don' you mind. Maybe—
well, maybe nex' year we can get a place."

CHAPTERS 29 AND 30

It settles down to steady rain, and the boxcar camp is bit by bit flooded out. First the people in tents flee the water; then those privileged folks in the boxcars watch with panic and indecision as the water rises around their vehicles and toward the floors of the boxcars: to leave, or to throw up a protective wall of earth and stick it out? The issue is somewhat accidentally decided by the beginning of Rose of Sharon's birth pains: the Joads must stay, and they convince the others to work at the wall. At first the man made levee successfully holds back the rising waters. Then disaster strikes (ironically, it is just after Rose of Sharon's baby has been born dead) in the form of sheer chance: a cottonwood is struck down by lightening, and its roots tear into the levee, and the water creeps, then flows through. Al dashes frantically to the truck, to try to start it and get it to higher ground; but he is too late, and the water has conquered them all. The rest is chaotic. Uncle John takes the shriveled little infant in the apple box and floats it down the floodtide, muttering in dull anger, "Go down an' tell 'em. Go down in the street an' rot an' tell 'em that way. That's the way you can talk. . . . Go on down now, an' lay in the street. Maybe they'll know then." Pa asks Ma, pleadingly, "Did we slip up? Is they anything we could of did?" Al's idea of tearing out the sides of the truck to build a platform on the floor of the boxcar, where they can move their stuff three or four feet higher and sit on top of it, out of the water, is put into operation. During the day and the night the families huddle on the damp platforms; in the dawn Ma asserts that they must go to higher ground. They start out through the deep water, the adults carrying the little ones on their backs and helping the weak Rose of Sharon. After walking along the highway they spot a barn and head for it. There is hay there. And in one of its corners there is a young boy crouching with his father. At Ma's request he offers a dirty comforter to dry Rose of Sharon. The little boy's answer to Ma's question about the deathly looking fellow with him is that he's starving. The boy explains bleakly that his pa hasn't eaten for six days: "Says he wasn' hungry, or he jus' et. Give me the food. Now he's too weak. Can't hardly move." The boy adds that when he realized the man was starving he stole some bread and made him eat it; but the man has not been able to keep the food down, and he needs soup or milk. Ma and her daughter exchange a deep look, and Rose of Sharon asks the rest of them to leave. They go into the tool shed. Then Rose of Sharon lies down beside the starving man and offers him the saving milk from her breast.

COMMENT

INTERPRETATION OF THE ENDING: As critics of Steinbeck have pointed out in some detail (especially Peter Lisca, *The Wide World of John Steinbeck*) the entire novel, and especially the ending, is filled with Biblical analogy and symbolism. The grapes, for example, have figured largely both as symbols of bitterness and of plenty (Lisca cites Biblical parallels: Revelation, Deuteronomy, Jeremiah, Numbers, Canticles). In particular Grampa before his death was continually evoking a vision of plenty through his allusions to the huge bunches of grapes he was going to devour when he got to California. It would seem that, as Lisca points out, Grampa "is symbolically present through the anonymous old man in the barn (stable), who is saved from starvation by Rosasharn's breasts. . . ." Two passages from Canticles bear this out: "This thy stature is like to a palm tree, and thy breasts to clusters of grapes"; (7:7) "I [Christ] am the rose of Sharon, and the lily of the valleys". (2:1) In giving new life to the starving man, Rose of Sharon is participating in a Christ-like way in the rebirth of a whole people (we recall here the ritual of communion, too—"Take, eat; this is my body. . . . drink, this is my blood"—symbolic spiritual rebirth through the symbolic absorption of Christ's body). We can say that Rose of Sharon comes to represent physical revitalization through Jesus Christ just as Jim Casey (whose initials are J. C.) stands for the philosophical prophecy of Christ. (Lisca cites analogues for Rose of Sharon's gesture in art, literature.

CHARACTER ANALYSES

THE JOAD FAMILY

GRAMPA: Grampa Joad is like a character out of Chaucers' "The Miller's Tale"—he is lecherous, loud, cantankerous, and the Joads seem to secretly relish his consistency in this. In the early pages of the novel he repeatedly insists on his intention to gorge himself on grapes when he reaches California. "Know what I'm a-gonna do?" he says. "I'm gonna pick me a wash tub full a grapes, an' I'm gonna set in 'em, an' scrooge aroun', an' let the juice run down my pants." Grampa is an old ripper, and his *joie de vivre* is earthily and convincingly pictured. Ironically, though, Grampa panics at the time of departure, has to be drugged with cough medicine, and dies of a sudden stroke on the first night out, to be buried on his homeground of Oklahoma.

GRANMA: She is Grampa's spirited equal, whether eating, cussing or praying. There is a characteristic anecdote told about her: once after a church meeting when she was talking in tongues she grabbed the shotgun and fired away part of Grampa's backside. This insured her rights with him for the duration of their long life together. Flighty as Granma appears, her affection for her husband is obvious in, for example, the chaotic moments in the Wilsons' tent before Grampa's death, when she hops about "like a chicken" shouting frantically at Jim Casy, "Pray, you. Pray, I tell ya. . . . Pray, goddamn you!" After Grampa's death she retires more and more into a dream world, until she dies in Ma's arms during the night as they drive across the desert.

UNCLE JOHN: Pa Joad's older brother, Uncle John can be regarded as the black sheep of the family, in that he is an eccentric loner, and a lonely guilt-ridden man. His story explains his actions: long ago his young wife, who was pregnant, had told him one night that she had a stomach-ache, which he ignored to the extent that he suggested she take some medicine. She died that night of a burst appendix. The pattern of Uncle John's life alternates between periods of severe abstinence and brief binges, alcoholic and sexual. Also, he has always tried to assuage his guilt by being good to people— candy and gum for the kids, a sack of flour dropped off on somebody's porch.

PA: The elder Tom Joad is a man who, when we meet him, is finding it hard to accept the brute fact of his eviction from the land, where he has labored all his life. His wife and children continue to show respect for him as the head of the family, but in point of fact the leadership slowly passes out of his hands into Ma's and Tom's. He is presented as a stunned, bewildered figure, sometimes angry, sometimes passive.

MA: Ma is a powerful though unassuming figure in the Joad clan. She is probably the ideal mother figure. She is patient in her unending labors, and in her determination to keep down fear and encourage joy in her family. She has a sense of humor and on occasion a kind of girlishness. Yet she can act, and act vigorously, in opposition to the menfolk when it is for the sake of preserving the family unit. Throughout the novel she emerges as a symbol of love, as a person who instinctively practices brotherly love. She is a person of insight and intuition, and is able to communicate with the philosopher of the novel, Jim Casy, and his unconscious "disciple," her son Tom.

NOAH: Nobody ever knows what Noah thinks or feels, or even whether he is slightly feeble-minded, as Pa fears, because of an accident at his birth. He does his work reliably and never raises his voice in anger. On the day before the family sets out across the desert, as they encamp by a river, Noah announces to Tom his decision to remain by the river and fish.

And indeed, the parting vision of such a placid existence for Noah is a natural one.

TOM: Tom is a central character, and perhaps the one who develops most—and survives—in the novel. He is individualistic and quick to anger if he feels he is being pushed around; he is also kind, sometimes witty, and potentially strong in the moral and intuitive sense that his mother is. In effect Jim Casy becomes his teacher, converting him by word and by his own example to the idea that a man cannot just look after himself but in the spirit of compassion is obligated to help others. Although he is still an outlaw of society at the end of the book, his status is actually changed: he is fighting for social amelioration, a better way of life for his people and for all struggling people. Tom, in other words, experiences re-education and rebirth in the novel.

ROSASHARN (Rose of Sharon):   In the four years of young Tom Joad's absence his sister Rosasharn grew up and married a local fellow, Connie Rivers. During the early part of the journey these two giggle and dream their way westward, as she carefully carries their unborn child. Most of Rosasharn's existence in the story is centered upon this child, who at length, because of inadequate diet, unsanitary and harrassing living conditions, and perhaps because of Connie's eventual desertion, is born dead in the last pages of the novel.

AL: Sixteen-year-old Al is expert at two things: tomcatting and mechanics. He worries about his responsibility for the old Hudson, but his judgments prove sound and dependable for the family. Typically, Al is an admirer of his older brother Tom and wishes to imitate him. At the end of the story he has become engaged to Aggie Wainwright, whose family has shared a boxcar with the Joads.

RUTHIE: She is 12, and seen in the novel at that point of suspension between girlhood and womanhood, ranging from ladylike composure which excludes her young brother Winfield to giggling, frantic games and exploits with him.

WINFIELD: He is 10, and realistically depicted in the gaucheries, the awkwardness, the mischievousness of a 10 year old.

OTHER CHARACTERS

JIM CASY: The ex-preacher is revealed from the first as an introspective man who retains the respect of the community in spite of—later, because of—the fact that he now refuses to preach. He has examined himself, he says, and has found that although he still strongly feels a call to lead and help the people, he can no longer in good conscience preach the religious gospel they are accustomed to. It emerges that he does not believe the old-time hell-fire and promise-of-heaven religion is realistic for their present needs. Jim Casy, who is the Christ-figure prophet until his martyr's death, speaks thoughts which reflect various philosophies: Transcendentalism, humanism, pragmatism, socialism. He does in fact lead and comfort the people; and he lays down his life for Tom Joad, who has in effect become his disciple and eventually takes over his work for social betterment.

MULEY GRAVES: He is a neighbor of the Joads in Oklahoma, and he represents one of the pathetic directions in which the ruined lives of the Okies ran. Although his family has migrated to California, "somepin' " kept him from accompanying them. The way he now roams the countryside, living almost like an animal off the land—"like an' ole' graveyard ghos'," as he confesses—he seems a little touched. He is a sad figure to all, as we get our final glimpse of him standing forlornly in the dooryard of the Joad homestead.

SAIRY AND IVY WILSON: This couple from Kansas link their fortunes with the Joads' on the first night out, when Grampa dies and they offer their help and possessions. Al fixes their car, and the families split their load into the two vehicles and travel on. Sairy Wilson is frail and ill, and in California, when they are ready to tackle the desert, it becomes apparent that she is at last too sick to travel. The

Joads unhappily leave the Wilsons behind, knowing that Sairy's death is imminent and Mr. Wilson's survival alone uncertain.

FLOYD KNOWLES: He is a young man who can be singled out from among the various men encountered by the Joads as a commentator on the conditions of the migrants. They meet him in the first Hooverville camp in California. He bitterly describes the exploitation of the workers by the owners, and the injustice and brutality of officials. His commentary is immediately borne out, for when a contractor comes into the camp looking for workers, accompanied by one of the innumerable deputy sheriffs, Floyd speaks up and demands his legal rights, and he is immediately arrested on the false charges of "red agitator."

THE WAINWRIGHTS: In that last of the Hooverville the Wainwright family shares a long boxcar with the Joads, while they all pick cotton. Al Joad begins to court their daughter Aggie and the two become engaged. Mrs. Wainwright assists in the birth of Rosasharn's stillborn child, and when the Joads leave to take Rosasharn and the children, Ruthie and Winfield, to higher ground, Al remains behind in the water-logged boxcar with the Wainwrights.

JESSIE BULLITT, ANNIE LITTLEFIELD, AND ELLA SUMMERS:
These women are members of the Ladies' Committee of Sanitary Unit Number Four who come to call on Ma in the Weedpatch government camp on their first day there. In their very human mixture of common sense, bustling self-importance, little personal jealousies, genuine good intentions and actual hard work they may be taken as prototypes of the figures who can be expected to rise to leadership and function effectively when the people are given choice and power.

MRS. ELIZABETH SANDRY: This woman should be mentioned as representative as a particular element which was a carry-over from the Bible evangelism, stomping and hollering religion from which the Joads emerged. A fanatical, sin-obsessed, spirit-stifling woman, she is not portrayed sympathetically. She viciously frightens Rosasharn with the contention that her baby will be deformed if she has "sinned" by "hug-dancing', and Ma tells her to be on her way. The manager explains to Ma that the woman will probably not bother them again; her system is always to call on and try to convert the newcomers to camp. We would find Mrs. Sandry among the "sin-mongers" who sit by in rigid disapproval of the Saturday square dance in the Weedpatch camp.

EZRA HUSTON AND WILLIE EATON: These men are chairmen, respectively, of the Central Committee and the Entertainment Committee of the Weedpatch camp. Here too their actions in warding off the riot attempt by outsiders at the Saturday night square dance may be regarded as symbolic of the progress which can be accomplished when the people run their own affairs. The survival of the good reputation of the camp—hence the survival of all the people there—was involved in the prevention of trouble that night, and the elected leaders of the people handled it.

JIM RAWLEY: Rawley is the humane manager of the government camp. In all his actions—from reassuring Ma about the intrusion by the amateur evangelist functioning as midwife in the delivery of babies—he behaves as a pragmatist (with common sense and a notion of realities) and a humanist (with compassion).

TIMOTHY WALLACE AND WILKIE WALLACE: These two men take Tom with them for a brief pipe laying job with Mr. Thomas right after his arrival in the government camp.

MR. THOMAS: Thomas is an interesting representative—a good man—of the small farmer or small businessman contingent in the hierarchy of laborers, owners, bankers, officials, etc. He is sympathetic to the situation of the migrants—for example, he himself is ashamed and angered that he must reduce their pay from thirty cents to twenty-five cents, and he does them the important favor of revealing the plan to cause a riot at the Saturday dance. He is one of the little men who will probably be squeezed out eventually by larger business interests; as it is, he is obliged to lower the wages because he is under the power of the Farmers' Association, which in turn is controlled by The Bank of the West. The power interests will not hesitate to wipe him out if he resists.

NOTE: As is obvious from a reading of the novel, there are innumerable faceless or nameless actors in the drama of *The Grapes Of Wrath:* i.e., the tractor drivers, the truck driver who gives Tom a lift, Mae and Al and the two truckers in the roadside restaurant, the one-eyed filling station attendant who hates his boss, the auto dealers, camp officials, sheriffs, storekeepers. All of them in a small way at least are to be regarded as commentators on the social situation in the novel.

CRITICAL COMMENTARY

STEINBECK AND HIS CRITICS: Much of the body of criticism of Steinbeck's writings has been founded on the first three of his novels to gain popular success and attention—*In Dubious Battle* (1936), *Of Mice and Men* (1937) and *The Grapes of Wrath* (1939)—which in a way is unfortunate, since it has caused critics to concentrate too heavily on the sociological content of those novels. One direction of Steinbeck criticism, then, has been concerned with his form of social protest, and in a larger sense, defining his "ideology." Another probably larger and perhaps more valid area of criticism has considered his "philosophy" (or philosophies), such as the biological view of man, non-teleological thinking, mystical symbolism. In a third category there have been critics— especially more recently, as the economic atmosphere of the thirties and the political furor of the forties, even the fifties, faded—concentrating on the measure of Steinbeck as creative artist, on an assessment of the literary value of his work in other words. [*Note:* The exact source of each critic's essay referred to in the following pages can be found in the bibliography at the end of the book.]

STEINBECK'S SOCIAL THEORIES: As suggested above, much of Steinbeck's work, following the lead of certain novels which doubtless did grow out of an economic and/or political situation, has been judged on sociological rather than aesthetic grounds. In so viewing his writings, critics have attempted to pin down Steinbeck's "ideology": their conclusions have ranged from socialism, agrarianism, Catholicism, to pro-communism and crypto-nazism. In 1942, for example, Maxwell Geismar considered Steinbeck, among others, in a book (*Writers in Crisis*) based on the premise that social consciousness is necessary for good literature; he finds that Steinbeck idealizes, but that the traits in his work which "fluster the

74

critics are those which endear him to mankind." It might be added that the definition of "social consciousness" to Geismar and to most critics who view literature sociologically is usually in line with their own socio-political thought; and the authors which most adhere to that line of thought (Geismar, for instance, is usually looked upon as a Marxist critic) are often most praised. Far afield from Geismar is a critique by John S. Kennedy which applies Catholic principles to Steinbeck (although his reading could just as well be regarded as "conservative Protestant"): Kennedy praises Steinbeck's versatility (most critics usually comment pro or con on this aspect of Steinbeck's work right at the outset of their essays, as if to get it out of the way because they hardly know where to place it in their argument) and the positive tone of what he sees as his "controlled socialism"; he defends him against the charges of pro-communism or crypto-nazism; but he finds that Steinbeck's elevation of the "group" over the "individual" and his tendency to "animalize" his characters (a reference to the "primitive" quality of many of his protagonists—Lennie the half-wit, Danny and his no-good friends—previously mentioned in the Introduction) shows a lack of human meaning. (If this sounds like arguing in circles, it is: critics often flounder on the paradox of Steinbeck's thought, that he has combined a very American sort of individualism with a concept of group action which approaches socialism. This combination has never been found very compatible with the popular conception—or misconception—of the democratic principle.)

An interesting and useful essay which does attempt to reconcile the above-mentioned paradox in Steinbeck's thought is Frederick I. Carpenter's "The Philosophical Joads," wherein he traces three strands of 19th century American philosophy as influences in Steinbeck's writings: American Transcendentalism, in its concept of the "Oversoul," and in its faith in the common man and in self-reliance (in other words, "individualism" as suggested above); secondly, Walt Whitman's almost religious elevation and love of the common man and his belief in mass democracy; thirdly, the pragmatism of William James, which stresses action, and judging life as it *is*, not as it ideally should be. Steinbeck's "religion," in other words, in such a book as *The Grapes of Wrath,* is "naturalistic" or centered on the human and the earthly [I have referred to it in the Plot Analysis and Comments, chiefly with reference to Jim Casy, as "humanism," which seems to be a more realistic term than "religion," since Casy is so concerned to reject his conventional religion and "preaching."]. Carpenter's essay is well-reasoned and valid. It is probably reinforced by an analysis of Steinbeck's "agrarianism," by Chester E. Eisinger in 1947, since Eisinger would add a fourth strand of American philosophy to Carpenter's three: "Jeffersonian agrarianism." Farming is a way of life, in which a man closely identifies with the land, with growth cycles; from his attachment to and love of the land he gains a sense of human dignity. By this same token the city and the machine are suspect—unproductive, inhuman, demoralizing. This critic goes on to question, however, the usefulness of such a philosophy in an increasingly industrialized and capitalistic society such as ours.

PUBLIC RECEPTION OF *THE GRAPES OF WRATH:* Martin Staples Shockley, writing in 1944, took the trouble to go back to where it all began, the furor over Steinbeck's social theories and ideology, in the reception of the controversial novel right after its publication. He treats the reaction in Oklahoma, but his survey may be considered representative of a whole nation's response and debate. Shockley also points out, importantly, that much of what passed for criticism in the early days of the novel's issue was in reality journalistic parry and thrust with the social problems underlying. One can get, incidentally, an excellent picture of the social milieu into which *The Grapes of Wrath* was dropped from Warren French's *A Companion to "The Grapes of Wrath."* Although Freeman Champney tends (like so many critics) to judge Steinbeck by one book, *The Grapes of Wrath,* his attempt to assess the geographical, cultural and economic influences on the author by going to live in "Steinbeck country" for several months is worthwhile. His assumption that Steinbeck accepted Marxism in the thirties, though, is challenged by other critics. At any rate, the debate about whether Steinbeck was—and/or still is—a social critic, and whether this limits or enhances his work artistically has continued down to the present.

BIOLOGICAL VIEW OF MAN & NON-TELEOLOGICAL, "IS" THINKING: In 1940 Edmund Wilson, along with others, started a rash of criticism aimed at discovering the essence of Steinbeck's "philosophy" in his admitted longstanding interest in biology (stated in the *Sea of Cortez* and as we have seen, closely connected with his deep friendship with Ed Ricketts, the marine biologist), and in his concept of what he called non-teleological or "is" thinking. Wilson, for example, pinpointed the "animalizing tendency" in Steinbeck: "Mr. Steinbeck almost always in his fiction is dealing either with the lower animals or with human beings so rudimentary that they are almost on the animal level. . . ." He found this to be an unfortunate influence on Steinbeck, amounting to "unsuccess in representing human beings"; or in other words, Steinbeck is deficient in characterization, according to Wilson. With the characters in *The Grapes of Wrath,* for instance, "it is as if human sentiments and speeches had been assigned to a flock of lemmings on their way to throw themselves into the sea." Wilson therefore finds what he calls the depiction of "almost unconscious processes of life" aimless, planless—and thus lacking in moral significance. Other critics, however, while they grant the animal-like substance of some of Steinbeck's characters, see it instead as a virtue, a "primitivism" which elevates what is *natural* or close to nature and out of which springs his "mystical symbolism."

"IS" THINKING VS. MYSTICAL SYMBOLISM: Here again critics have floundered on what they see as a conflict between "is" thinking—what we have referred to as Steinbeck's pragmatism—and the need for value judgments in the human world, along with what seems intuitive and mystical in Steinbeck's work. Significant essays which treat this problem in one way or another were produced by Stanley Edgar Hyman, Woodburn Ross and Frederick Bracher. Hyman, who is also to be considered a somewhat sociological critic, detects the relationship of the individual to society as integral to all Steinbeck's work. Hyman tends to identify Steinbeck with his characters, that is, making them spokesmen for himself; also, he sees in Steinbeck the view that nature is good and man evil, hence his "primitive" type characters. Writers such as Ross and Bracher manage more or less to combine happily Steinbeck's naturalistic and his humanistic tendencies. That is, Steinbeck likes the natural, scientific world which caused his intense interest in marine biology, detailed observation of nature; at the same time Steinbeck finds a larger significance in nature—plants and animals and natural cycles of growth and change—which he relates to man in an intuitive and mystical way. In other words, asserts Frederick Bracher for example, Steinbeck in his biological view of man is not *equating* men with animals (this is often referred to as "animalism," as a reduction of man to a lower level, and it is the chief source of the adverse criticism Steinbeck's theory has received: Steinbeck dehumanizes man, these critics say) but is rather elevating them through a kind of mystical reverence for "life in all its forms." Basically, these critics are asking, can naturalism and mysticism exist side by side in an author's work? It seems to them to be a paradox. Bracher, with Hyman and Ross, concludes (though more sympathetically than derogatorily) that Steinbeck "never really resolves some of the paradoxes involved in a non-teleological approach." Bracher's essay of 1948 is well-informed and clarifying on many issues of Steinbeck criticism. Another excellent essay by Woodburn Ross titled "John Steinbeck: Naturalism's Priest" (Ross had previously written "John Steinbeck: Earth and Stars," examining the so-called conflict between naturalism and mysticism) seems to continue Bracher's thought. [Naturalism, we might point out, is generally assumed to forego moral or ethical considerations or commentary; it is a form of "is" thinking in that it merely observes, putting down facts as they are. Although this is a misconception about naturalism, since most naturalist writers have always written from an ethical foundation and had an ethical end in view, it is the crux of the troubled debate about John Steinbeck's naturalism versus his mysticism.] Ross really follows up Carpenter's significant essay, too, in his assertion that there are ethical implications in Steinbeck's naturalistic writings (hence, "naturalism's *priest*"). Ross says that Steinbeck has "succeeded in taking the materials which undermined the religious faith of the nineteenth century and fusing them with a religious attitude in the twentieth, though a religious attitude very different from what the orthodox in the nineteenth century would have thought possible. Nature as described by the scientist becomes not merely the foundation of a revolutionary ethic; it also supplies . . . the basis of a sense of reverence. . . . Steinbeck is, I think, the first significant novelist to begin to build a mystical religion upon a naturalistic base. . . . It abandons all attempts to discern final purposes in life. It virtually reduces man again to animism; for, unlike Wordsworth, Steinbeck does not see through nature to a God beyond; he hears no intimations of immortality. . . . There is only nature, ultimately mysterious, to which all things belong, bound together in a unity concerning whose stupendous grandeur he can barely hint. But such a nature Steinbeck loves, and before it, like primitive man, he is reverent." Ross's reference to 19th century thought can be assumed to include Carpenter's "three strands" of Transcendentalism, Whitmanesque humanism and Jamesian pragmatism; there is also probably Eisinger's agrarianism. As some critics would point out in disagreement with Ross, however, in his statements such as "he hears no intimations of immortality," he seems to ignore the strong urging (through Jim Casy and then, Tom Joad) in a novel like *The Grapes of Wrath* for the concept of an Oversoul—one big soul—which is certainly founded more in religion than it is in nature. (The American Transcendentalists may have stressed the realization of the Oversoul through nature; but Steinbeck makes it very clear that for Jim Casy the idea has been channeled through his religion, and is an elevation not a reduction of man and his aspirations.)

AESTHETIC EVALUATIONS OF STEINBECK: Joseph Warren Beach's two chapters in his book *American Fiction 1920–1940* are representative (in a superior way) of the trend in Steinbeck criticism which, finally, turned to aesthetic problems —that is, what kind of creative artist is Steinbeck? what is the literary value of his writing? In "John Steinbeck: Journeyman

Artist," which considers the fiction up to *The Grapes of Wrath,* Beach is refreshingly undisturbed by so-called inconsistencies (such as the paradox of naturalism and mysticism which bothered the above-mentioned critics): in a reasonable and sympathetic manner he goes about treating Steinbeck's supposed intentions, his special subjects, his written style, the question of his realism (naturalism) and his symbolism and then assigns him rank in literary accomplishments where he feels such praise is in order. One weakness he attributes to Steinbeck—if it can be termed weakness—is that he sometimes confuses art and life (this sounds a little like what has been said by some critics of Charles Dickens' work, that it contains too much life and too little art; other critics would add, though, that in the case of either or both writers, these two—art and life—are hardly irreconcilable). Beach calls *The Grapes of Wrath,* though (in "John Steinbeck: Art and Propaganda") "perhaps the finest example so far produced in the United States of a proletarian novel." For the unity of that novel of epic proportions, Beach reinforces the point made in above Comments, that Steinbeck's method of "interchapters" helps to unify the themes, symbols, action of the novel. Beach also finds Steinbeck's characters more credible and moving than many critics.

More recently, in 1954–1955, the issue of art or propaganda in *The Grapes of Wrath* was renewed, in a debate in *College English* between Bernard Bowron and Warren G. French. In a somewhat limited and perhaps unfair article Bowron assesses the continued popularity of the novel as Steinbeck's "calculated exploitation of perennial formulae of the western story genre" (his article is titled *"The Grapes of Wrath*: A 'Wagons West' Romance"), and contends it is not great art. Warren French, Steinbeck's biographer, defended the author against such charges, arguing that the genre of migration and search for a "promised land" is a very old one (a point supported by the Biblical analogy mentioned herein: the Israelites in Egypt, exodus and the land of Canaan), and that Steinbeck's characters are not "primitivistic escapists." Perhaps the most interesting aspect of the above debate was the letter on criticism from John Steinbeck himself, written at the request of the editors of *College English* that he comment on the controversy. This letter reveals Steinbeck's continuing distrust of the intellectualism which takes the form of pedantry and sterile hypothesizing in criticism; Steinbeck says, for instance, "I wish I could so comment but I have no opinions nor ideas on the subject. Indeed, both pieces seem to me to be nearer to taxonomy than to criticism. Much of the new criticism with its special terms and parochial approach is interesting to me, although I confess I don't understand it very well, but I cannot see that it has very much to do with the writing of novels good or bad. . . . the new critics fight each other even more fiercely than they do the strapped down and laid open subjects of their study. . . ."

PETER LISCA ON STEINBECK: It is fitting to conclude with the comments of a writer who has become an expert on Steinbeck, through his *The Wide World of John Steinbeck* (which is an expansion of his doctoral thesis) and other articles, and through contacts with Steinbeck himself. (The reader will recall that Lisca has been quoted from throughout this study.) In concluding his study of Steinbeck, Lisca remarks that "perhaps Steinbeck's most significant accomplishment has been the new dimensions he has given to the materials of literary naturalism," materials which "have led Steinbeck not only to experiment with all aspects of form, but to assert man's divinity." Thus we see that Lisca can be placed among those critics who do not shy away from the "inconsistencies" or paradoxes of Steinbeck's thought, from the biological view of man and non-teleological, "is" thinking to ideas of intuitive knowledge and mysticism. He quotes Steinbeck from *Sea of Cortez,* to good purpose: "Why do we dread to think of our species as a species? Can it be that we are afraid of what we may find? That human self-love would suffer too much and that the image of God might prove to be a mask? This could be only partly true, for if we could cease to wear the image of a kindly, bearded interstellar dictator, we might find ourselves true images of his kingdom, our eyes the nebulae, and universes in our cells." As Lisca points out, Steinbeck's "study of nature through the discipline of marine biology led him to a reverence for life in all its forms." (This has been referred to as humanism in the above study.) Of Steinbeck's versatility, which has covered experimentation and range of subject matter, point of view, philosophical attitude and variety of prose style, Lisca concludes that such versatility represents craftsmanship, a very vital quality in an artist, and asserts, "It is this craftsmanship which has enabled Steinbeck, almost alone among the writers of his generation, to give permanent aesthetic values to the materials of the Great Depression: in *Of Mice and Men* a symbolic construct of man's psychological and spiritual as well as his social condition; in *In Dubious Battle* an impartial, cold, but powerful analysis of the struggle between labor and capital; in *The Grapes of Wrath* what constitutes, in theme, purpose, scope, and language—an American epic.

ESSAY QUESTIONS AND
ANSWERS FOR REVIEW

QUESTION: 1. Discuss the idea of a Transcendental "Oversoul" as it appears in the novel.

ANSWER: It is Jim Casy who first brings up, in folk idiom, the concept that, translated, resembles the Oversoul propounded by the American Transcendentalists, especially Ralph Waldo Emerson. The Transcendentalists defined "Oversoul" as a sense of oneness with God, with nature and with other individuals. The discovery of the Oversoul had to be made through intuition; that is, a person felt or sensed this truth, rather than saw it as a tangible fact. Jim Casy, the ex-preacher who has been doing a lot of thinking, because he has found the religion of Bible-belt evangelism no longer adequate to his needs or the needs of his people. He has come up with the idea that the "spirit of God"—for in his country any version of religion has always included the idea of "spirit" and "getting the spirit"—may be instead the human spirit. And instead of separate souls, every single person's soul—and I believe the word *spirit* can be used synonymously—may go to make up part of "one big soul." At several points in the novel he renews the discussion of one big inclusive soul that holds together, unites all people. It can be seen that such an idea also fits in with the concept of the family unit and the social philosophy of group action developed in the book.

QUESTION: 2. What would you say is the social philosophy developed in *The Grapes of Wrath?*

ANSWER: Theoretically viewed, it is probably based upon the ideas of Marx and Lenin and other socialist thinkers of the past and present. Yet the social philosophy which develops in this novel is also peculiarly American, founded on what might be termed loosely "the American Dream": the principle of democracy, of course, including the rights due to all under such a system; the pioneer spirit of endurance which first explored and settled the Middle West and the West; the will to forge ahead and succeed—drive (even though the undesirable effects of this same urge are revealed in the form of grasping materialism and ruthless power interests in the novel). Specifically, the social theory which develops and is realized in action in *The Grapes of Wrath*—through the efforts of the Jim Casys, the Tom Joads and those who choose to follow them— is that which urges that the small people, the poor people, those most in a position to be exploited and denied by the power of the profit hungry, must amass strength through banding together and taking group action. As the novel progresses, this idea first takes the form of worried, angry conversations among the frustrated men: "We have guns. What if we banded together to fight the owners, the banks, the deputy sheriffs?" There are some past examples before them—i.e., the mountain men who revolted successfully in Akron, Ohio against rubber companies. There is the present working example of the essentially socialist community of the government camp at Weedpatch: there the people manage all their own affairs—government, economy, policing, health, recreation (along the lines of the modern Israeli *kibbutz*)—and they also keep out unwarranted intrusion and intimidation from outsiders to the camp. "Advanced" social theory (for the period under consideration—the depression and post-depression years) is also realized, at length, in that the jobless and starving men come to understand the nature of "unions" and "strikes," along with the violence of "strikebreaking," unfortunately. At the end of the novel Tom Joad, who has killed a deputy sheriff in defense of Jim Casy, brutally murdered for his "agitation" for a union and for strikes to get fair wages, has set forth to work toward this same social ideal. For the one ruthless social lesson learned by the Joads and their like in the novel is that "separately we are weak, together we have strength."

QUESTION: 3. Briefly describe the biographical and historical background which produced *The Grapes of Wrath*. Given this context, how was the novel received at its publication, and more recently?

ANSWER: First of all, John Steinbeck knew intimately the country and the people about which he wrote. Born and raised in the Salinas Valley in California, he lived most of his first forty years there (and much of his writing until recently was set in that locale). Furthermore, in the mid-thirties he became aware of and disturbed about the conditions of migrant workers in general (he had observed them in his own countryside, in California) and the plight of those who were forced to flee from the Dust Bowl of parts of Kansas and Oklahoma in particular. He wrote newspaper articles on the subject in 1935 and 1937, having gone to Oklahoma and made the westward trek to California with the migrant workers themselves. (The latter series of articles was published as a pamphlet called *Their Blood Is Strong*.) It needs hardly be added that other published commentary of the period—excepting that which defended certain ownership and public interests in the states most involved, such as California and Oklahoma—corroborates Steinbeck's journalistic findings which he metamorphosed into fiction.

At its publication in 1939 the novel was received essentially as a social document and a work of social protest, by both its admirers and its detractors. It was acclaimed, even in the form of a Pulitzer Prize to Steinbeck; it was widely discussed and debated in newspapers, magazines and on the radio; it was of course turned into a movie; and it was in some places banned and burned, for its so-called revolutionary socio-economic theories (for the charge of "Red!" was as panicked, as all-inclusive and as vaguely defined at that period of American history as it has been in more recent years), for its so-called unfair and untrue report of the conditions of migrant laborers, and for its so-called dirty language.

When some of the first furor over the novel died down, however, critics began to look at it from an artistic point of view and to ask the question which is still being asked and answered pro and con—is it art or propaganda? Or, in fact, does one have to choose between the two? Critics of each decade since its publication have tended to look upon it with the going critical attitudes and habits of their group, with a general shift from the sociological readings toward artistic critiques which include everything from Steinbeck's various philosophies (humanism, pragmatism, biological theory of man, non-teleological thought, agrarianism—how well these come across in the context of the novel), his alternations between the dreamlike and the real (fantasy, allegory, symbolism), his ideas of good and evil, the individuality or universality of his characters, his mystical symbolism.

QUESTION: 4.   How can the word *humanism* be applied to *The Grapes of Wrath?*

ANSWER: All the major characters in the novel, with Jim Casy and later, Tom Joad leading, seem to move from a religiously based to a humanly based philosophy of life in the novel. It is clear, of course, as soon as Jim Casy begins to explain to everyone why he cannot be a "preacher" any longer that he more and more finds the religious precepts of his and his people's immediate past untenable in their present realities: some of Jim's most memorable speeches early in the book are his declarations that he wants to help and comfort the people still, he feels things are changing and they are going someplace, but he can no longer look upon sin in the conventional Bible-belt evangelical way nor can he offer facile prayers or parade future heavenly glory to people whose lives are materially and psychically wretched in the present. In another important speech he claims the "sperit"—a feeling of which has always figured so largely in local religion—seems now to him to be more of a *human* spirit than the spirit of a remote God; at any rate it is this human spirit which he now feels sure of, just as he feels certain that the souls of all the people go to make up one great soul: the Oversoul spoken of before.

Tom Joad moves toward a philosophy of humanism in the novel, too. At the beginning, although he is a sensitive, kind and communicative person, he is still, rather naturally, "out for himself"—individualistic, we might say, focusing on his own personal and material well-being and of course, the welfare of the Joad family. His actions, that is, stem more from particular causes and crises rather than from any sense of general principle. As he says, "I put one foot down in front of the other," and "I climb fences when I got to climb fences." He is, however, an admirer and disciple of Jim Casy's almost from the beginning, too, since Jim is the first person from his past whom Tom encounters on his way home from prison. Tom always listens with curiosity and interest to Jim Casy, and later he realizes, as he tells his mother, that he has absorbed more of Casy's philosophizing than he knew. He takes over Jim Casy's philosophy and his tasks, too, at that point after Casy's martyrdom when he quotes the preacher and takes up his credo that "Two are better than one." He speaks in terms of "our people," of doing something so that they may live decently and happily again. Tom Joad has thus enlarged his compassion to all human beings, beyond the family unit.

The women like Ma and Sairy Wilson can of course be included among the "humanists" in the novel too, for (first of all as mothers) all their actions are outgoing and predominantly selfless. Ma Joad cares about human beings and understands them strikingly well. There are countless examples of her insight and understanding: after Grampa's death, later in the evening, she instructs Rosasharn to go and lie by Granma because "she'll be feelin' lonesome now"; she is constantly attuned to the complex emotions which come with Rosasharn's pregnancy, compounded by the desertion of her husband Connie—Ma prevents Tom from needling her, yet encourages her to see Tom's jokes about her swelling body as affectionate, which they are; she comprehends that the girl in her loneliness wants to enjoy the Saturday dance at Weedpatch but desperately fears the temptation of her flesh, so that she and Ma go and sit together, Rosasharn secure in Ma's promise to keep her out of trouble; and at the very lowest ebb of her daughter's morale, shortly before her baby is due, Ma makes exactly the right move by giving Rosasharn the gift of gold earrings, one of the few family possessions salvaged, and further distracts her from her troubles by piercing her ears on the

spot. Ma silently and without judgment whatsoever acknowledges Uncle John's absolute need to get drunk on the night
Jim Casy has stepped forward to go to prison in place of Tom;
on another occasion, she breaks down with reasonable and
sympathetic words the pathetic defenses of the mother whose
hungry children have licked the Joad stew pot and gone home
to brag and ask questions about it. One of the prime instances
of Ma's insight into and compassion for humanity is her exchange with the scared little storekeeper at the Hooper ranch,
where her hard-earned dollar is so swiftly absorbed by the
exorbitant prices set by the Hooper controls. She has com-
plained with perfect justice about the unfair price on each
item of her purchases. When finished shopping and on her
way out, she realizes that she still has no sugar, which she has
promised the family. She asks the man to trust her for the
dime's worth of sugar, which her family is earning at the
moment out in the orchards. He cannot: company rule. Not
even for a dime, Ma asks? "He looked pleadingly at her. And
then his face lost its fear. He took ten cents from his pocket
and rang it up in the cash register. 'There,' he said with relief." While he cannot go against the owners, out of fear, he
can loan money from his own pocket. As Ma gratefully
acknowledges his huge gesture, in relative terms, she makes her
point about "humanism" among the poor people in general:
"I'm learnin' one thing good. Learnin' it all a time, ever' day.
If you're in trouble or hurt or need—go to poor people.
They're the only ones that'll help—the only ones."

It might be added that the humanistic philosophy we find in
The Grapes of Wrath has been attributed to the influence of
Transcendental philosophy, which stresses man's worth and
dignity and potential depth of character, and to Walt Whitman's
exuberant belief in the masses and love of one's fellow man.

QUESTION: 5. What is meant by the application of the
term "agrarian philosophy" to The Grapes of Wrath?

ANSWER: Such a philosophy, or thematic strain, which
has been linked to what is known as Jeffersonian agrarianism—

a form of democracy and a way of life—is everpresent in the novel. That is, Steinbeck elevates farming as a way of life, if it is accompanied by love of, respect for the land. For those who love the land and make it a way of life it takes on symbolic meaning: the people identify with cycles of natural growth and contrastingly, when the soil erodes and is worn out it is at the same time the spirit of the people eroding and wearing out. Ideally, then, the land can be a unifying thing, holding people together and bringing serenity and well-being— and importantly, a sense of human dignity. As it is said at one point in the novel, "I am the land, the land is me." But likewise, if the land is taken away, then a man's identity—and so his self-esteem—is taken away. And if the people are uprooted from the land, then their unity is destroyed, proven in the novel as we witness the disintegration of the Joad family unit. One of the most eloquent pleas for agrarianism comes in an interchapter late in the novel, wherein the spring and the exquisite ripening of all growing things in California is described, then harshly and bitterly contrasted with the wilful destruction of nature's perfections by those who care only to make profit from the orange or the grape—what the author calls the shopkeepers and manufacturers of the land, who have replaced, for profit's sake, the genuine farmers.

QUESTION: 6.   How can the word *pragmatism* be related to *The Grapes of Wrath?*

ANSWER: Pragmatism is generally considered to be one strand of the philosophy found in the novel. As Steinbeck has himself put it, it is also referred to as "non-teleological" or "is" thinking. It means, in brief, looking at things and trying to evaluate them and act upon them as they really *are* instead of as our various preconceived notions or theories tell us they *should* be (hence the distrust of certain conventional "shoulds" of religion in the novel, and their replacement with the realities of human existence and need, "is" thinking). Jim Casy, Tom Joad, Ma are all in varying degrees examples of pragmatists: they try to look at life as it really is, without invariably applying standards they have learned somewhere, which are often inapplicable (the many questions about what is or is not "sin" which arise and are resolved through personal reasoning and judgment rather than by preconceived rules illustrate the pragmatic direction of thought in the novel); they are also flexible, noticing the details of one situation which make it different—hence its result or resolution different—from another. At one point, for example, Ma declares that she will take things as they come (when Al has asked her if she is scared about the new life), she will do what she has to do when something happens to require her action: this is exactly the rule of action she adheres to throughout. The shouting religionists say it is a sin to get drunk; yet Uncle John, in his life and deeds one of the kindest men known, sometimes finds it absolutely necessary to his psychic survival to go on a drunk—Ma, as we have seen, does not condemn such an action. Or, for another example, Ma carefully adjusts her behavior in the progress of the Joad family disaster toward Pa, by custom and right the head of the family but by necessity a figure more and more regarded as passive: Ma notes each alteration, judges and acts accordingly. Jim Casy has looked around him, and "listened to the people," as he so often says; and from what he has seen and heard he has had to change his notions of what "sin" is: fleshly pleasure, for instance, especially among people who work hard, assume family responsibilities, help their neighbors, suffer sometimes incredible hardships, he no longer can look upon as sinful. All that is a part of life must be taken into the consciousness and dealt with; and life is various.

QUESTION: 7. Comment briefly on symbolism in *The Grapes of Wrath*.

ANSWER: The dust, the turtle, and the grapes can be singled out, and two characters in particular—Jim Casy and Rose of Sharon. The dust symbolizes the erosion of the land and the erosion of the lives of the people. As we see at the beginning of the novel, it has pervaded, discolored, choked and ruined everything. The dust of course is synonymous with "deadness." The land is ruined, a way of life is shattered, and the lives are uprooted. More remotely, the dust also stands for the profiteering owners in the background, who are "dead"— i.e., indifferent—to the life and love of the land, and who are the ultimate cause of the change from fruitful to barren soil. The soil, and the people, have been drained and exploited. (We might hazard a guess that the rain at the end of the novel, which is of course excessive, in a way completes the cycle of the dust, which was also excessive. In this way nature has restored a balance and has initiated a new growth cycle. This ties in with other examples of the "rebirth" idea in the ending.)

The turtle, which appears and reappears several times early in the novel, stands for survival, for the driving life force in all mankind. For the turtle ploddingly but steadily advances past every obstacle he encounters: the red ant in his path, the truck which tries to crush him, being imprisoned temporarily in Tom Joad's jacket (and he advances, incidentally, toward the southwest, the direction of the mass migration). Also, the turtle is consistently pictured as ancient, lasting, almost primieval; horny head, yellowed toenails, indestructible high dome of a shell, humorous old eyes.

The grapes seem to symbolize both bitterness and plenty (and critics have found Biblical analogies—of both line and situation—for these ambivalent meanings). The title of the novel of course is taken from the song, "Battle Hymn of the Republic," which evokes in image and in feeling an invincible army marching on to victory. And so the Joads and their brothers, in their increasing frustrations and sufferings, are depicted, as an army growing in ever more militant wrath toward an irrevocable demand for restitution and comfort. Granpa, the oldest member of the clan, is the chief spokesman for the grapes as symbols of plenty: all his descriptions of what he is going to do with those luscious grapes out in California vividly suggest largesse, content, freedom.

It has been suggested by critics that the old man (although not so old as Granpa was when he died) who receives sus-

tenance from Rosasharn's breast at the end is a kind of sur-
rogate, or substitute, for Granpa; and since he is saved from
starvation, hence from death, this constitutes a rebirth for the
Joad clan (Granpa being the actual "father") and for the
whole people figuratively viewed. In line with this view we
have Rosasharn as not only a mother giving nourishment but
almost a Christ-figure (there is a passage from Canticles re-
ferring to Christ as Rose of Sharon, and suggestive of revitalization; the notion of rebirth through Christ's physical body
is of course symbolized in the ritual of communion, also, with
the "bread" and the "wine" which stand for Christ's body and
his blood). The clearest figure of the Christ-like prophet, of
course, is the philosophizing Jim Casy. His symbolic function
can be verified in a number of ways: the initials of his name,
of course; his continual soul-searching, culminating in what
he himself refers to as his time in the "wilderness" when in
prison; his life as an example of what he comes to believe;
the discipleship of Tom Joad toward him, which he hardly
solicits but which Tom seeks in the light of his goodness; the
substitution of his own body—symbolically, his life—for Tom's
to go to prison, to "save" Tom (since for him to go to prison,
having broken parole, would be disastrous); and finally, his
actual death, which is in essence a martyrdom for the people
whom he has lead and comforted and fought for, in which he
paraphrases (as he has previously done) the last words of
Christ on the cross: "They don' know what they're doin'."

QUESTION: 8. Comment briefly on John Šteinbeck's
style of writing.

ANSWER: In general, Steinbeck seems to alternate between
passages of description (frequently included in short separate
chapters called interchapters) and narrative consisting of dialogue and action. The descriptions are often filled wtih exquisitely observed detail, whether of nature or of the material,
man-made world or of human nature. There is a great variety
of style in *The Grapes of Wrath,* and it has been attributed
to a number of influences, of which the following seem valid:
the Bible, particularly the Old Testament (this is substantiated

by the fact of the many paraphrases and analogues to the Old Testament in the novel); American poets such as Walt Whitman and Carl Sandburg; John Dos Passos and his so-called "newsreel technique" (the chapter treating the used car dealers, for example); the chanting, repetitive technique of the chorus in Greek tragedy; and of course the folk idiom itself, from which the dialogue is realistically reproduced.

BIBLIOGRAPHY AND GUIDE
TO FURTHER RESEARCH

Beach, Joseph Warren. *American Fiction: 1920–1940*. New York, 1941. Contains two worthwhile essays, dealing particularly with Steinbeck from an aesthetic point of view.

Bowron, Bernard. *"The Grapes of Wrath*: A 'Wagons West' Romance." *The Colorado Quarterly,* III (Summer, 1954), 84–91. A derogatory essay proclaiming that Steinbeck writes in stereotypes and facile generalizations.

Bracher, Frederick. "Steinbeck and the Biological View of Man." *The Pacific Spectator,* Winter, 1948. A useful essay on this facet of Steinbeck's thought.

Carpenter, Frederick I. "The Philosophical Joads," *College English,* 2 (January, 1941), 315–325. See also "John Steinbeck: An American Dreamer," *Southwest Review,* 26 (July, 1941), 454–466. This critic is dealing chiefly with what he sees as Steinbeck's version of "the American dream."

Champney, Freeman. "John Steinbeck, Californian," *The Antioch Review,* Fall, 1947. Based on a stay of several months in Steinbeck's California country.

Eisinger, Chester E. "Jeffersonian Agrarianism in *The Grapes of Wrath,*" *University of Kansas City Review* (Winter, 1957), pp. 149–54. A discussion of Steinbeck's agrarian thinking in our industrialized society.

French, Warren. *A Companion to "The Grapes of Wrath."* New York, 1963. A very interesting and useful collection of background material to the novel, ranging from a definition of "Okies" to a discussion of the movie.

———————————. *John Steinbeck*. New Haven, Conn., 1961. Biography.

Geismar, Maxwell. *Writers in Crisis*. Cambridge, 1942. Contains an essay which treats Steinbeck's career as a search for social values.

Gerstenberger, Donna and George Hendrick. *The American Novel 1789–1959*. Denver, 1961. Contains an extensive list of articles on *The Grapes of Wrath*.

Griffin, Robert J. and William Freedman. "Some Persuasive Motifs in *The Grapes of Wrath*," *Journal of English and German Philology*, July, 1963.

Hoffman, Frederick J. *The Modern Novel in America*. Chicago, 1951. Essay on Steinbeck.

Hunter, J. Paul. "Steinbeck's Wine of Affirmation in *The Grapes of Wrath*," *Stetson Studies in the Humanities Number One*. Deland, Fla., 1963.

Hyman, Stanley Edgar. "Some Notes on John Steinbeck," *The Antioch Review*, June, 1942. A sociological reading.

Kazin, Alfred. *On Native Grounds*. New York, 1942. Essay on Steinbeck.

Kennedy, John S. "John Steinbeck: Life Affirmed and Dissolved," in *Fifty Years of the American Novel*, ed. Harold C. Gardiner. New York, 1951.

Lisca, Peter. *The Wide World of John Steinbeck*. New Brunswick, N. J., 1958. Lisca's book, an expansion of his doctoral dissertation and a useful, informative critical study of Steinbeck's work, has established him as an expert.

McElderry, B. R. Jr. "*The Grapes of Wrath*: In the Light of Modern Critical Theory," *College English*, V (March,

1944), 308–313. An attempt to determine whether the book is art or propaganda.

Modern Fiction Studies, Autumn, 1964. An entire issue devoted to articles on Steinbeck and up-to-date bibliography.

Pollock, Theodore. "On the Ending of *The Grapes of Wrath,*" *Modern Fiction Studies,* IV (Summer, 1958), 177–178.

Ross, Woodburn. "John Steinbeck: Naturalism's Priest," *College English,* 10 (May, 1949), 437–438. A perceptive essay on Steinbeck's biological theory.

Shockley, Martin Staples. "Christian Symbolism in *The Grapes of Wrath,*" *College English,* 18 (November, 1956), 87–90.

Steinbeck, John. *The Grapes of Wrath.* (first publication, 1939) Viking Press Compass edition, New York, 1958.

Taylor, Walter Fuller. *"The Grapes of Wrath* Reconsidered," *Mississippi Quarterly,* (Summer, 1959), pp. 136–44. Sums up the case against religious and economic philosophies behind the novel.

Watt, F. W. *John Steinbeck.* New York, 1962.

Wilson, Edmund. "The Californians: Storm and Steinbeck," in *Classics and Commercials.* New York, 1950. Also found in his *The Boys in the Back Room.* This essay, first published in 1940 and a fairly negative critical assessment of various qualities in Steinbeck's work (what is called his naturalism, or animalism, for example), was very influential to several decades of Steinbeck criticism which seemed to follow Wilson's lead.